AF521801

Sally Gall

Heavenly Creatures

Sally Gall

Meditation by Eric Fischl

Heavenly Creatures

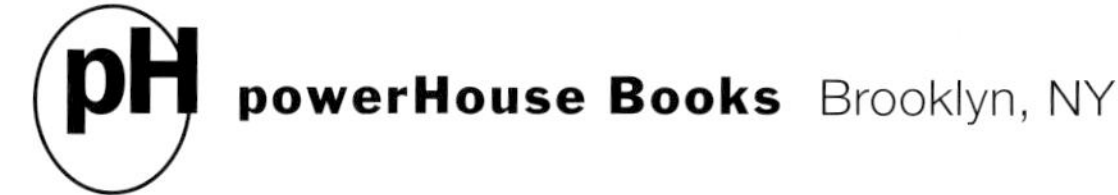
powerHouse Books Brooklyn, NY

Heaven on Earth: Sally Gall's New Photographs

Though my meditation on Sally Gall's new body of photography, which involves kites and clotheslines, is not about painting, I must start there. I'm starting at that moment in art-historical time when photography usurped painting's authority as arbiter of direct and verifiable observation.

To some painters, this moment of usurpation meant liberation, freeing the hand and the eye to look elsewhere for truth. To others, it was condemnation and relegation to a diminished status—a life of effort they no longer needed to exert.

Ironically, the liberation of painting from the constraints of "objective" reality, which allowed it to move away from the surface of things and into a deeper and more abstracted "feeling" realm, brought painting literally back to the surface. Painting became first and foremost about paint.

Several years ago I visited Monet's home in Giverny, France, the site of so many of his greatest contributions to the history of art. This is the place where he finally got rid of the horizon line and let the water lilies scatter across the surface of the painting to become compositional and tonal markers on an inflected surface of paint. This is where Monet almost gave up trying to capture detail.

His estate has tried diligently to recreate his famous garden so that when walking through it you can crop your sightlines in ways that give you the impression that you are witness to his moment of inspiration. I stood before his iconic pond, full of its blossoming water lilies, anchored at one end with his oft-painted Japanese footbridge. I stared. I squinted. I cupped my hands beside my eyes to block out peripheral distractions. I could see what was there. I could see what he chose to paint. What I could not see was what he saw.

If you are too tethered to the practical eye, the familiarity of objects stand no chance of becoming inspired, animated, fantastic and strange; no chance for transformation.

A principle difference between painting and photography, when artists reach to capture the essential shapes and colors that will push their perception towards abstraction, is that painting breaks free while photography always includes elements of its source.

One could argue, rightfully, that the transformative experience in art is more difficult to achieve through photography because it is always moored to its own banality.

So, when a photographer is able to achieve an ecstatic and animated transformation from what, until that photograph was made, had passed as unremarkable, you have to acknowledge that photographer is not just skilled but truly gifted.

Sally Gall has always been interested in waves and caves, caverns and curls, folds and furls. In her most recent work, she continues to express her delight and pleasure in the sensuality of form, specifically the flickering of things in the breeze.

This book, *Heavenly Creatures*, weaves together two stories, both having to do with wind, air, and colorful shapes, but to this she brings a new perspective: these stories can only be seen from below.

Kites on strings and clothes on clotheslines appear as abstract shapes set against a ground of blue, luminous yet flat. Sally has done for laundry and kites what Karl Blossfeld did for plants: transcend their natures while absolutely adhering to them.

Let me change the subject. (As I said, this is a meditation so I'll allow it to go where it pleases.)

There are two kinds of art making, paradoxical in their oppositions but contained within the creative mind. An artist is generally predisposed to one or the other. On the one hand, you have art seeking to resolve pain, torment, injustice, emptiness, and conflict through truth-telling. On the other, you have art that blatantly disregards that suffering.

During WWII, while Matisse painted the sensuous glow of the Mediterranean sea and sky, the color saturated folds and patterns of an odalisque's garment, and the curves of her glowing skin, his wife and daughter were picked up by the Gestapo for questioning. I put it to you to tell me which painting he was working on at the time of this grave interruption.

Clearly, either Matisse did not feel that stress and worry, or the darker emotions were not the best fuel for his inspired practice. He had his eyes set on the distant horizon: the site of ultimate conflict-resolution. Through the lightness of his touch, the light of his color, the eroticism of his fluid lines, he delivered to us a near-heavenly pleasure that carried us out of the temporal, out of our suffering, out of ourselves.

Sadly, I am not that kind of artist, but Sally Gall is. In these dark days of American existential conflict and crisis, where anger and fear are running fast and burrowing deep, it has to be seen as an act of bravery to turn one's attention away from the flame and focus their net on capturing the elusive distractions of fleeting beauty.

From Zbigniew Herbert's poem, Ornament Makers, I take these few lines because it is in these lines that the significance of Sally Gall's art is most eloquently expressed.

Praised be the ornament makers
the masons and the decorators
the creators of flitting angels…

the poets it goes without saying
the defenders of children playing
giving voice to smiles hands and eyes

they're right it is not art's business
to seek the truth is for science
masons guard the heart's warmth

Eric Fischl, Sag Harbor, New York, August 1, 2018

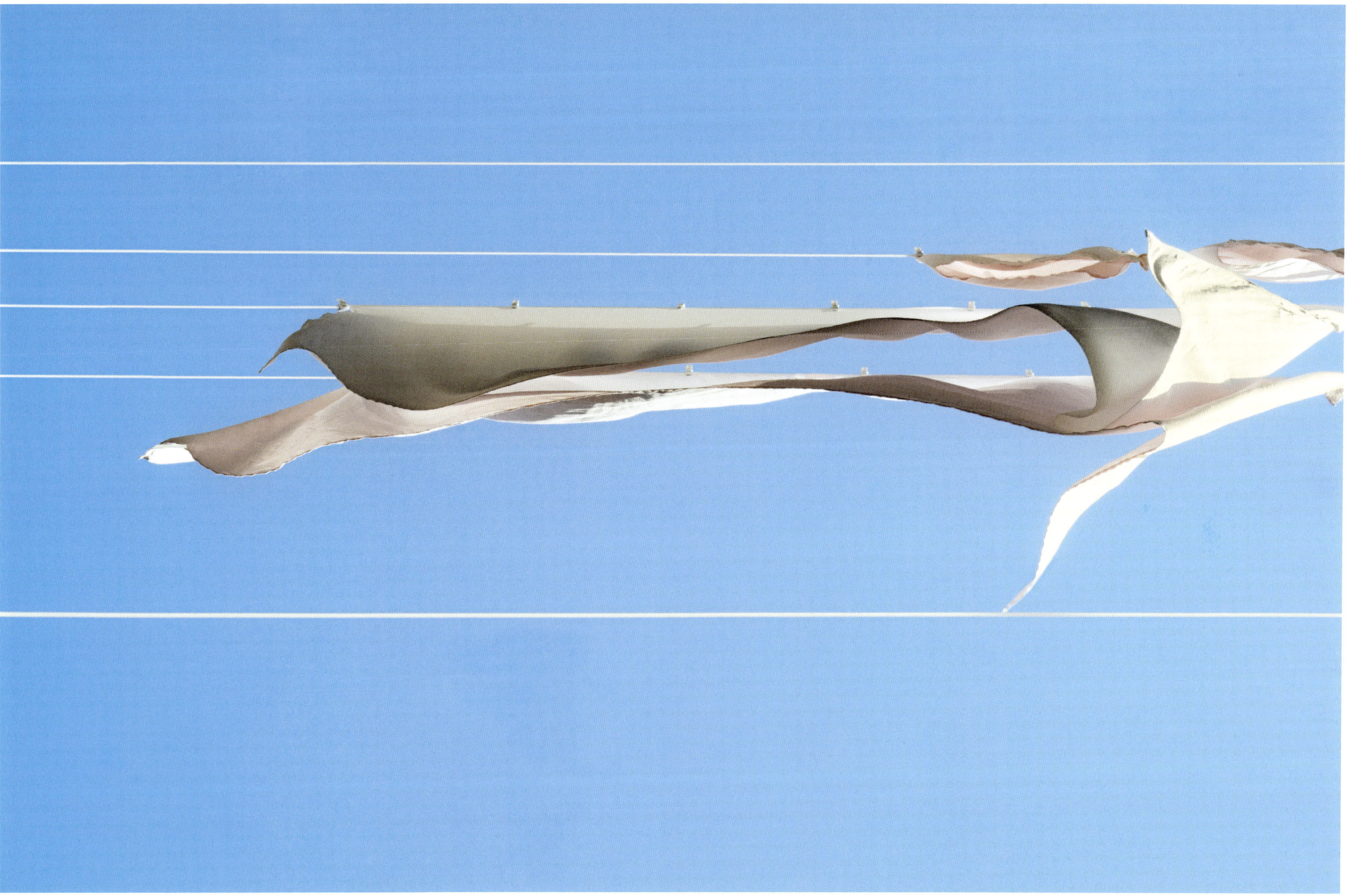

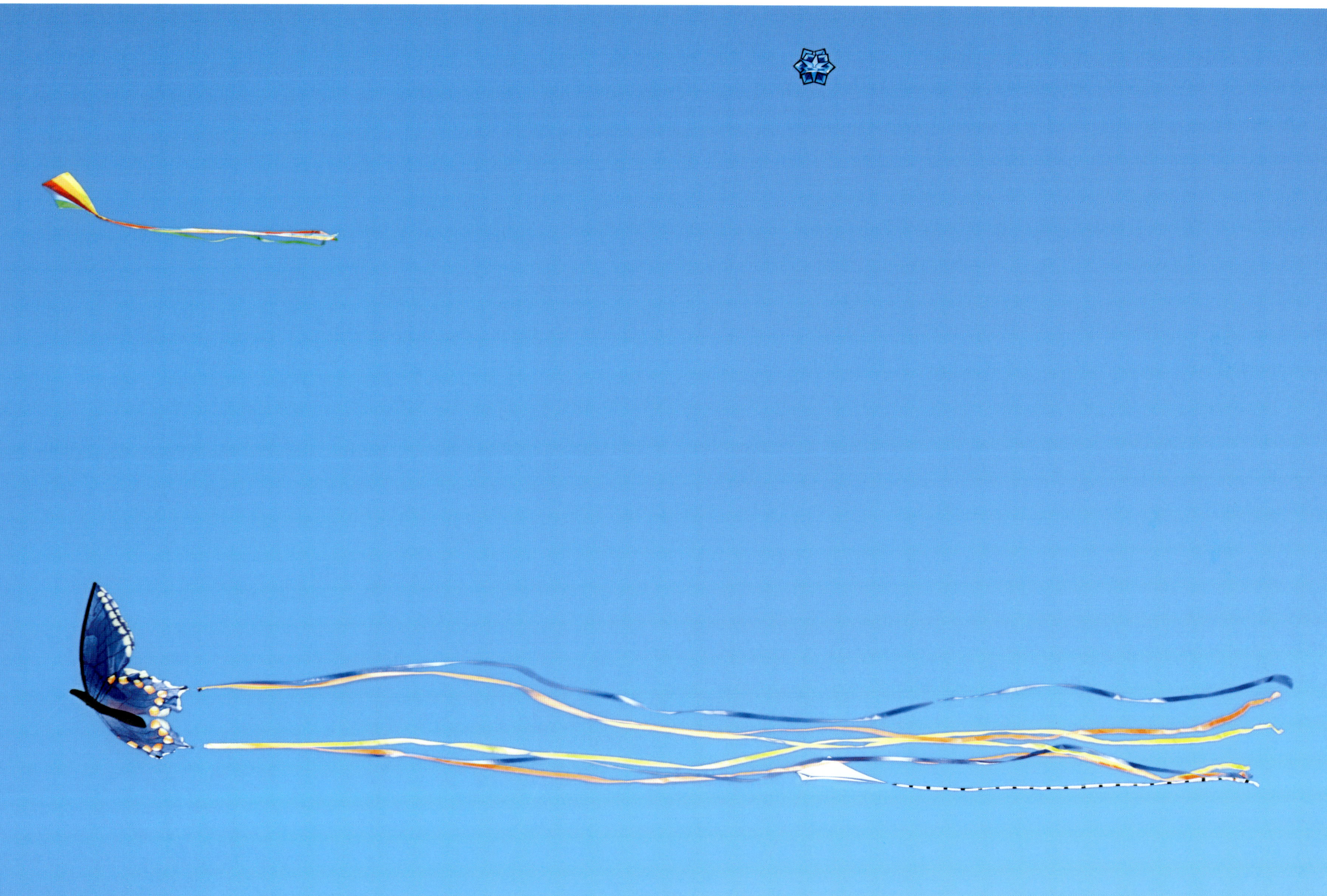

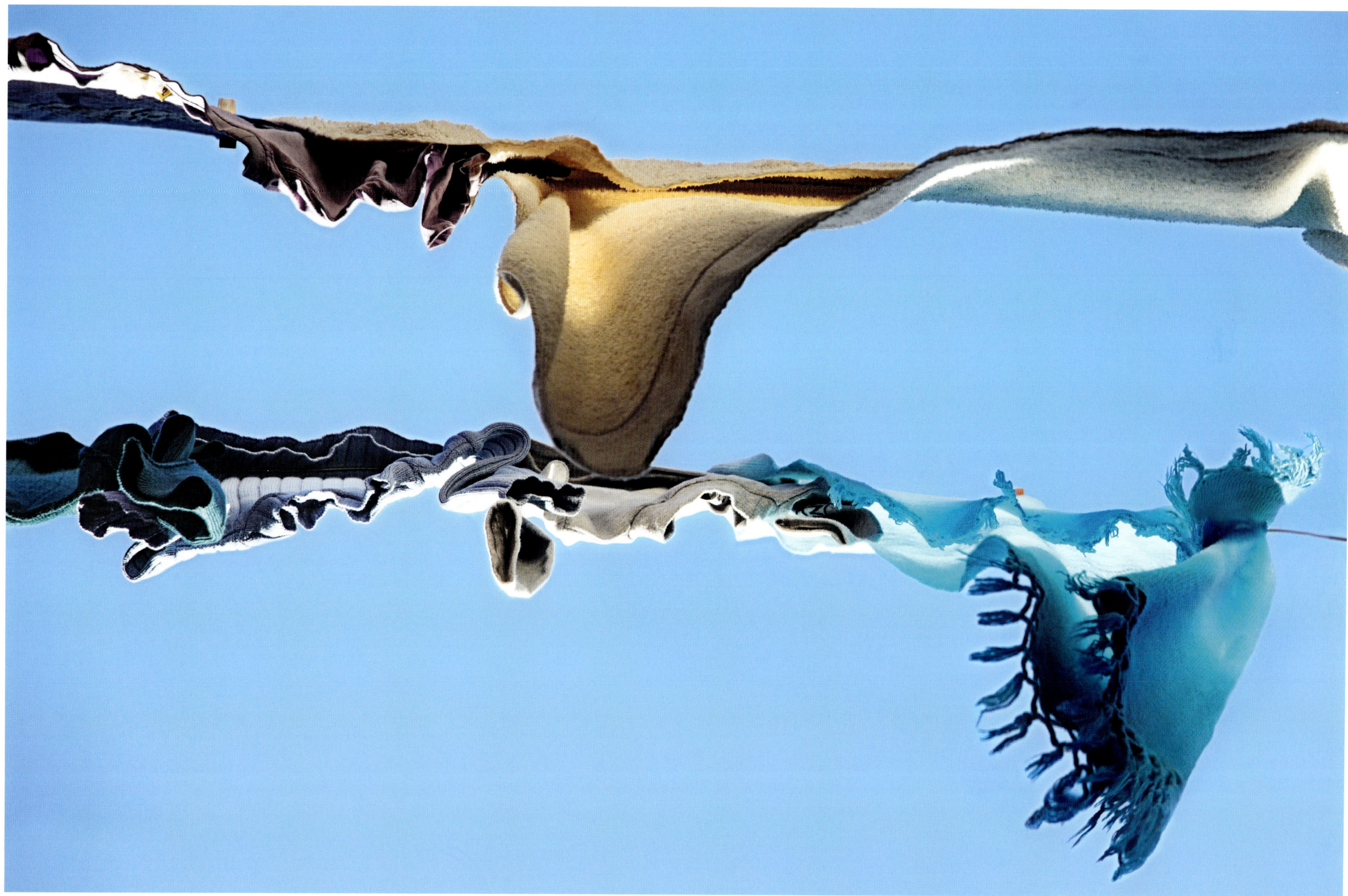

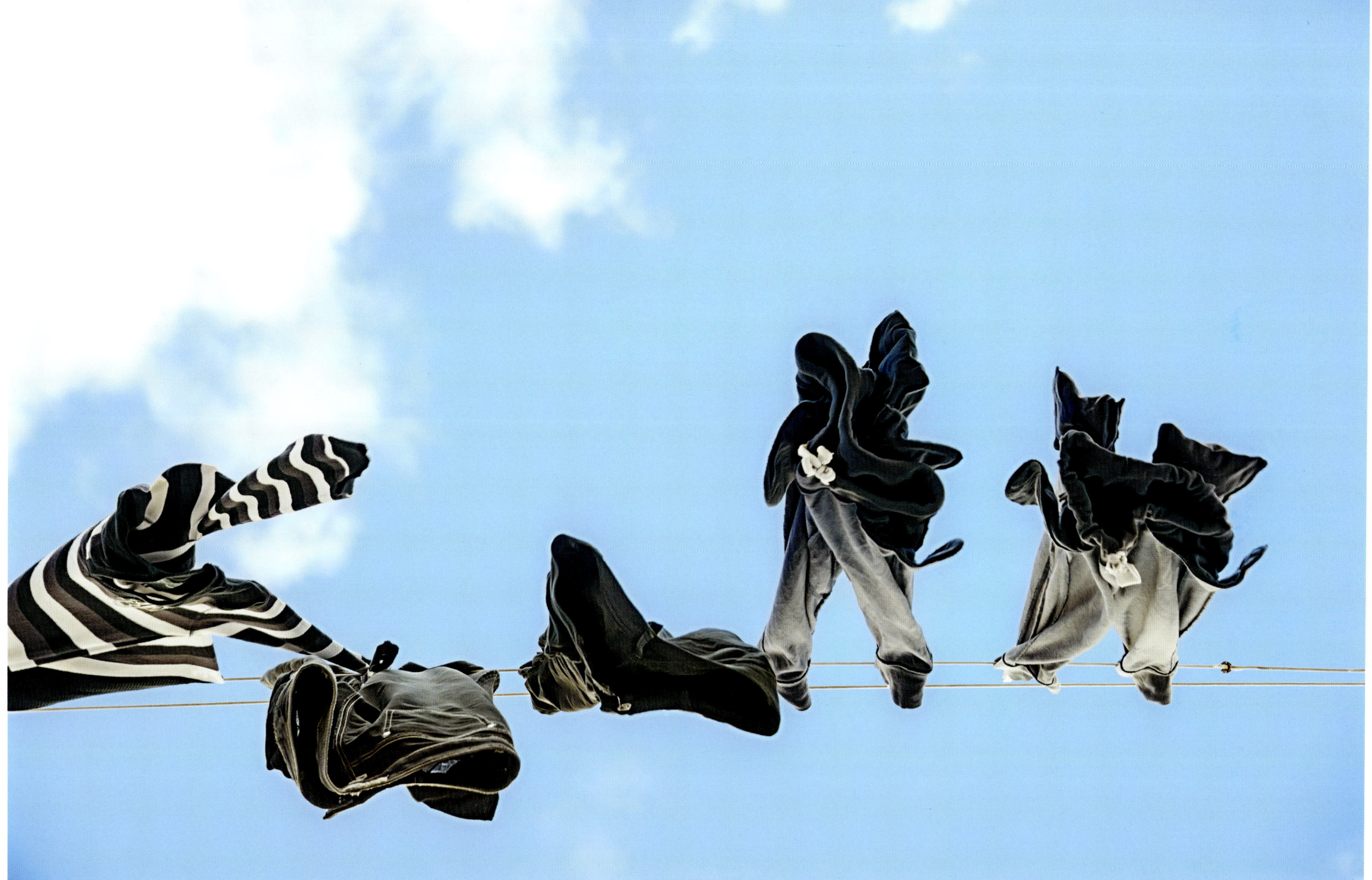

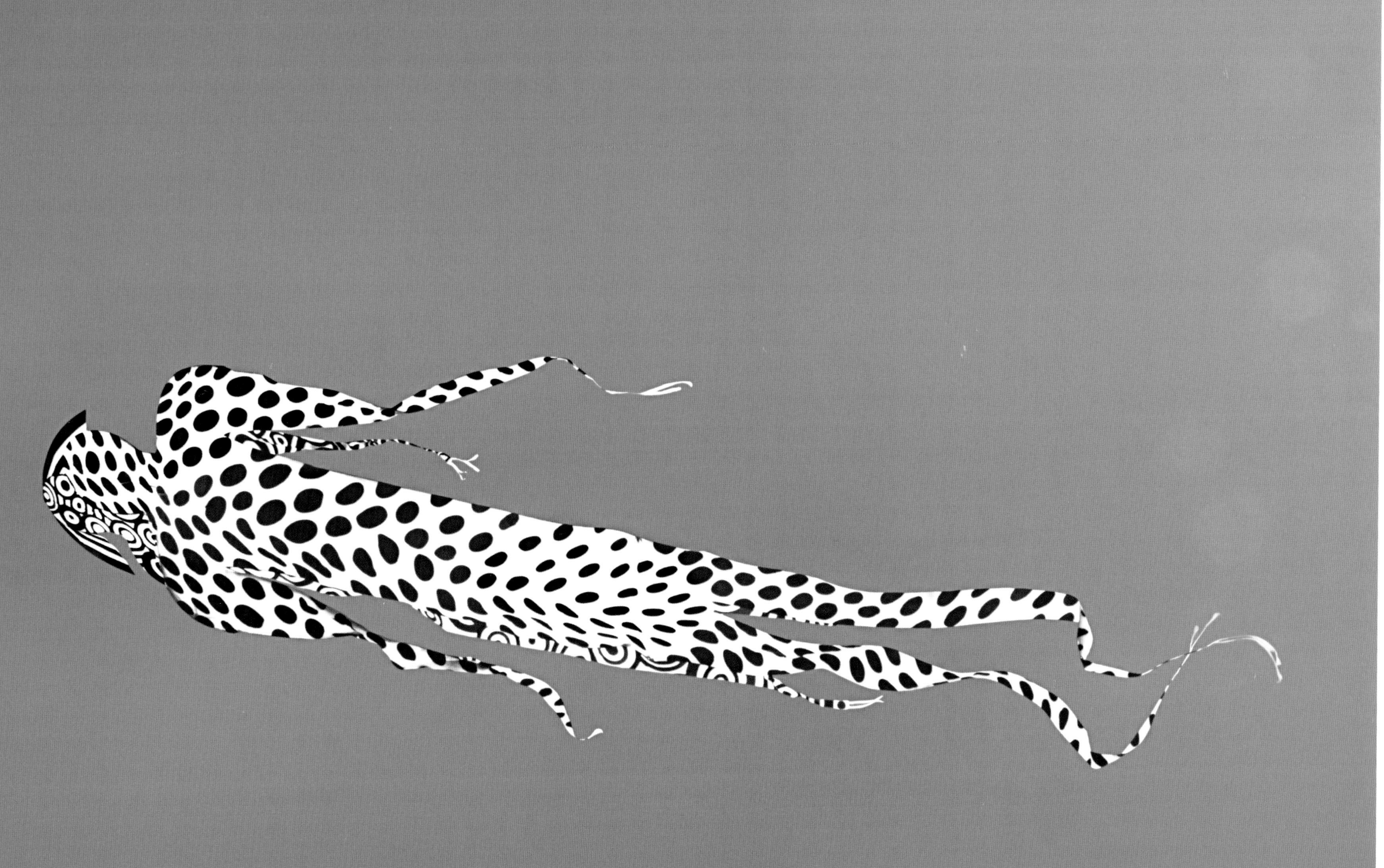

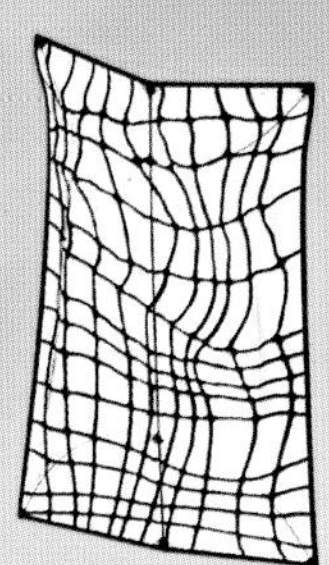
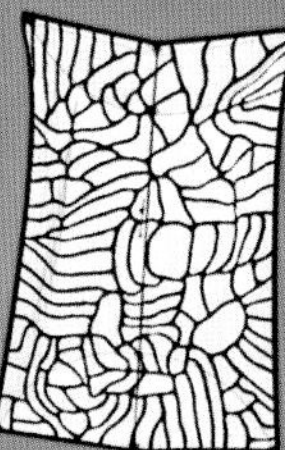
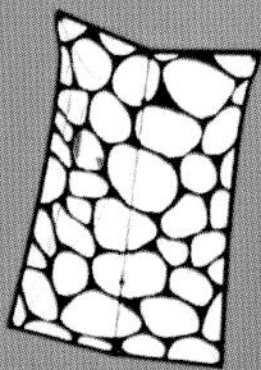

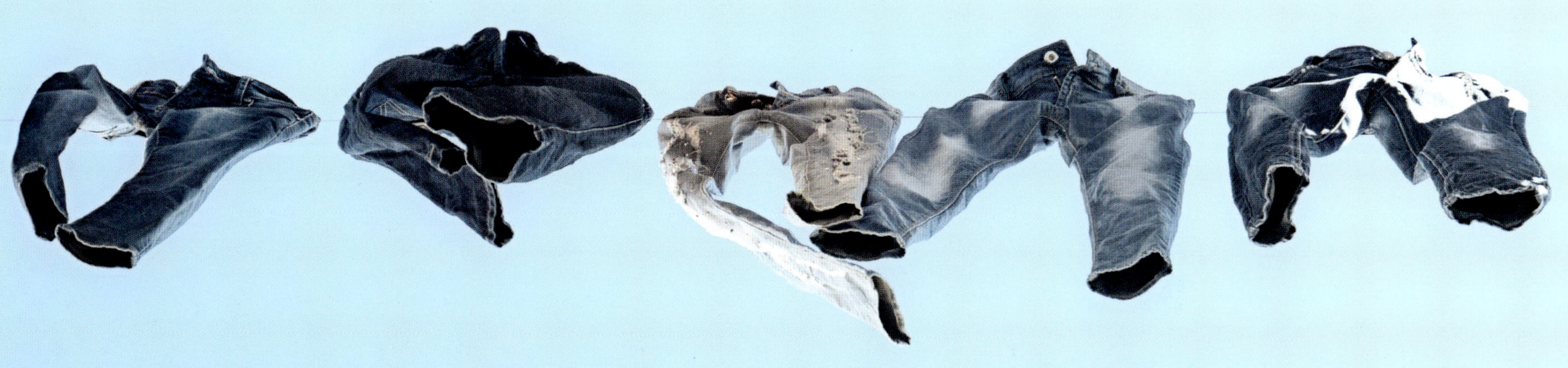

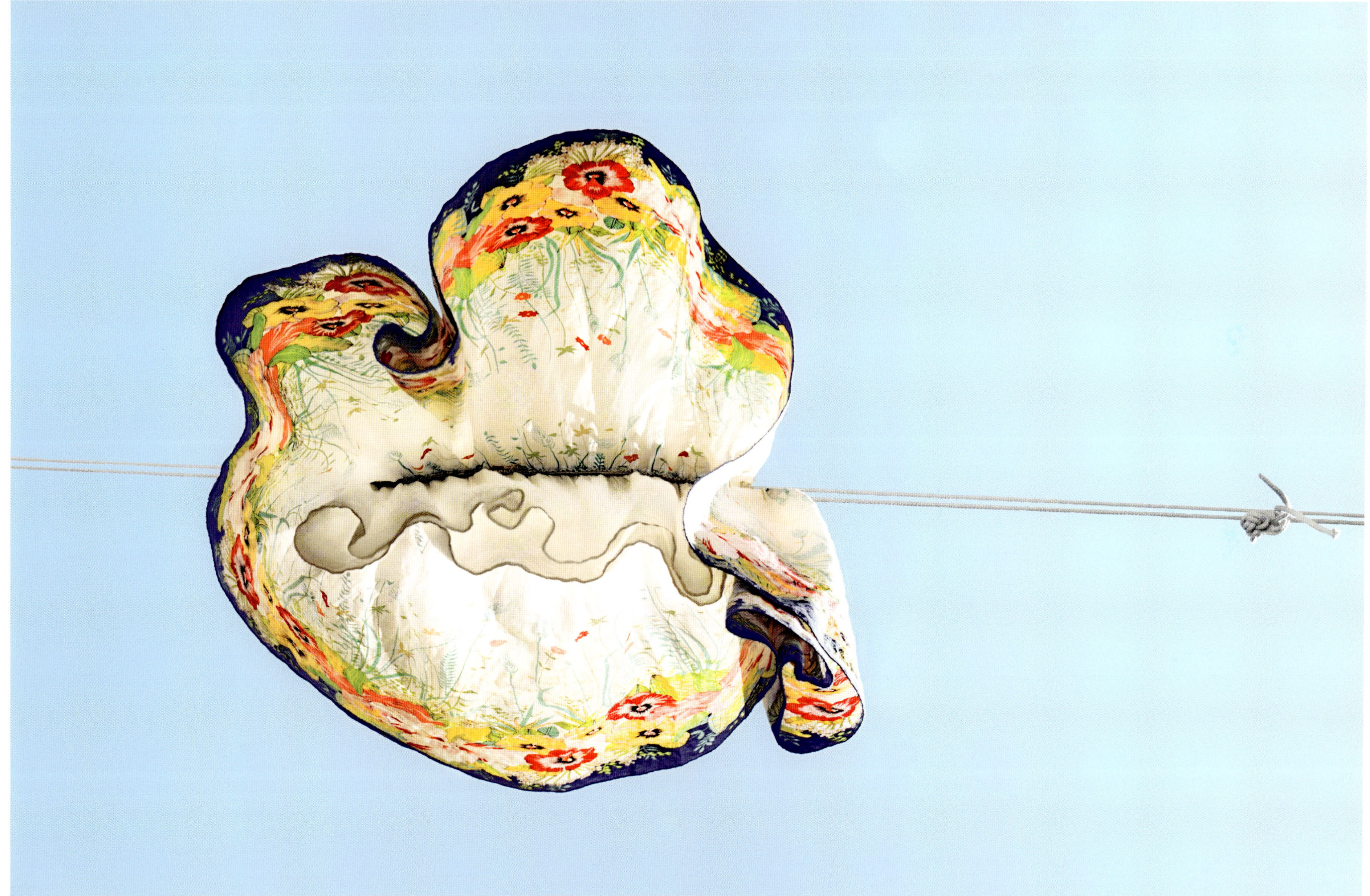

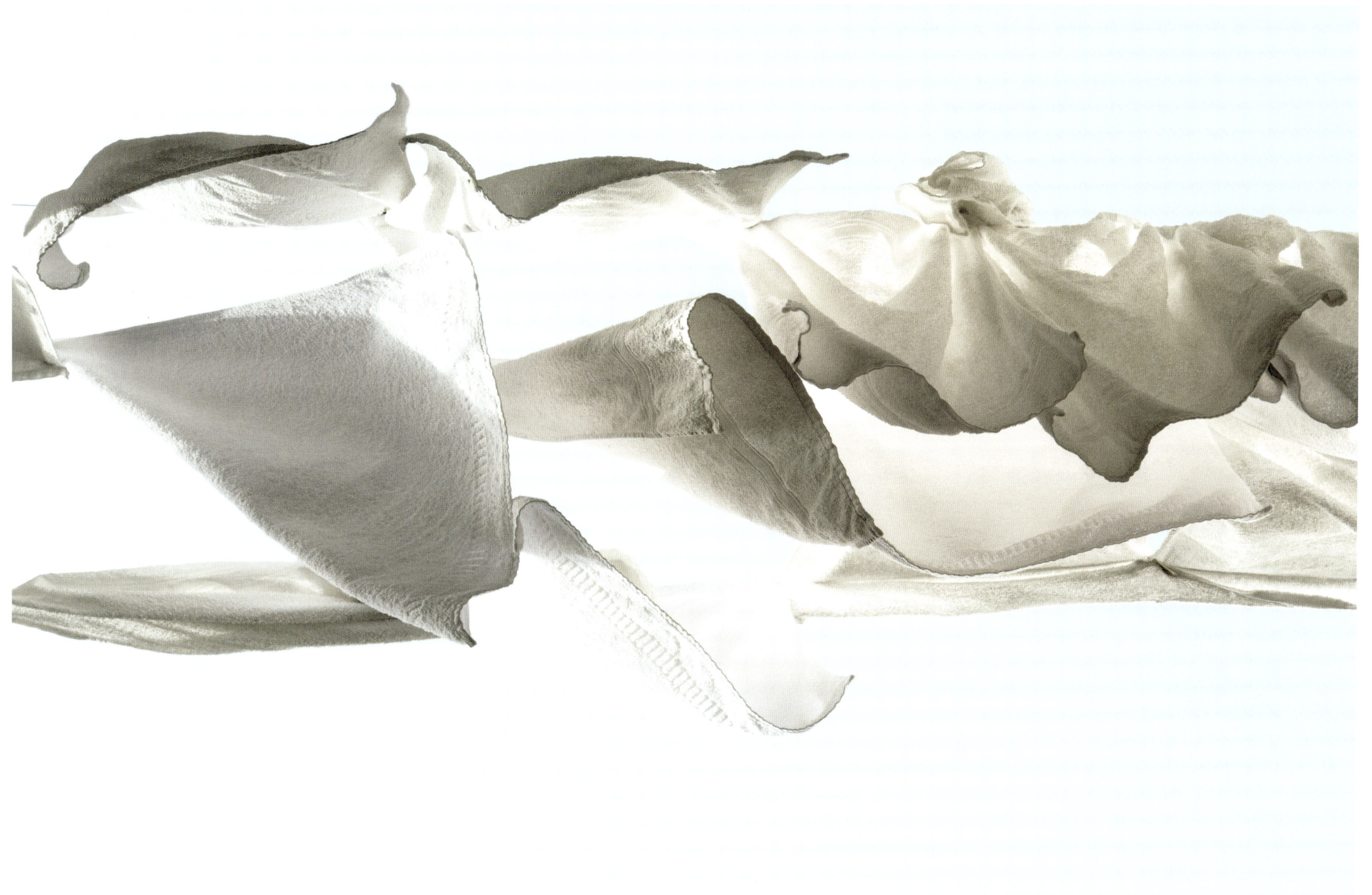

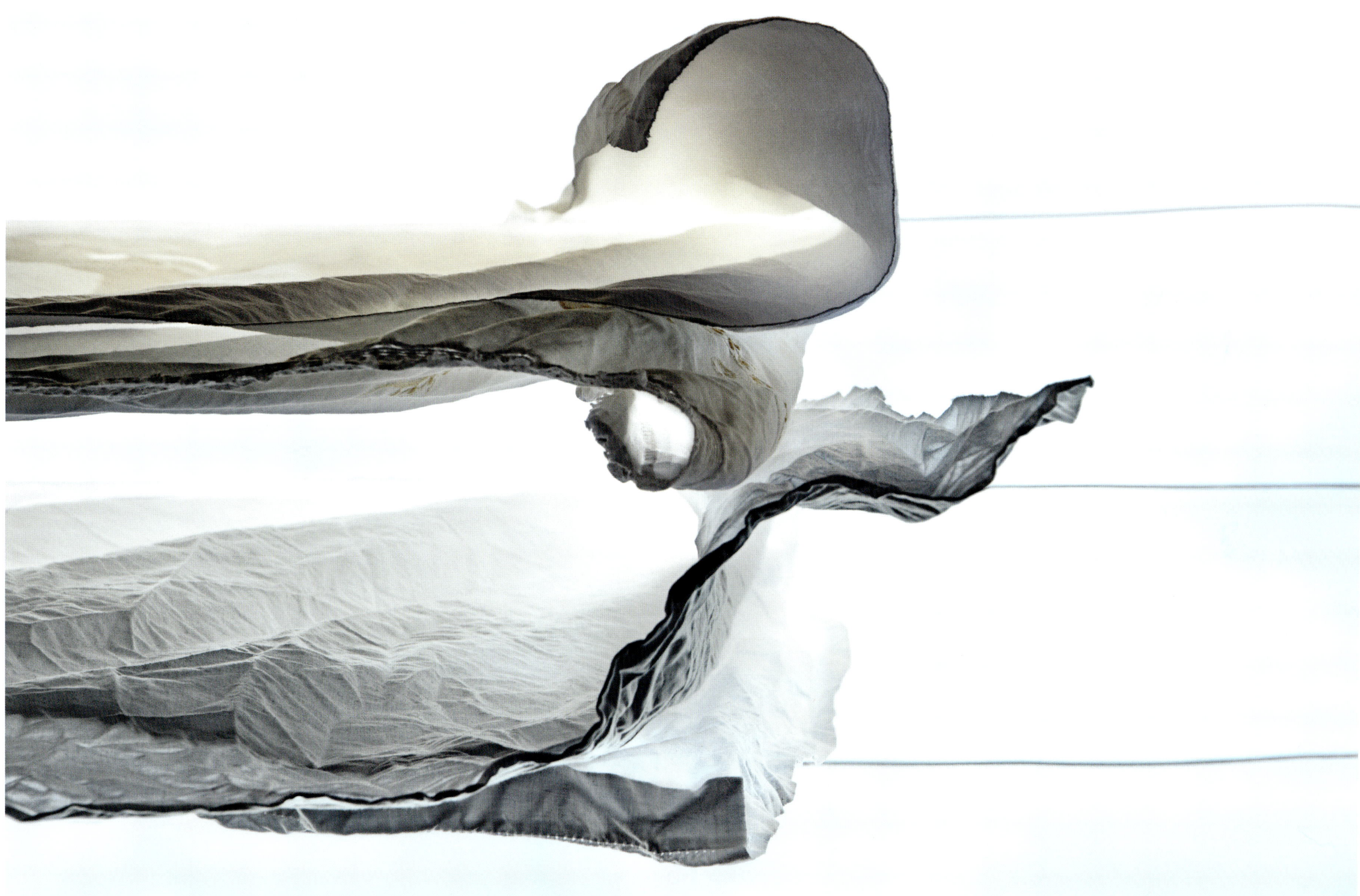

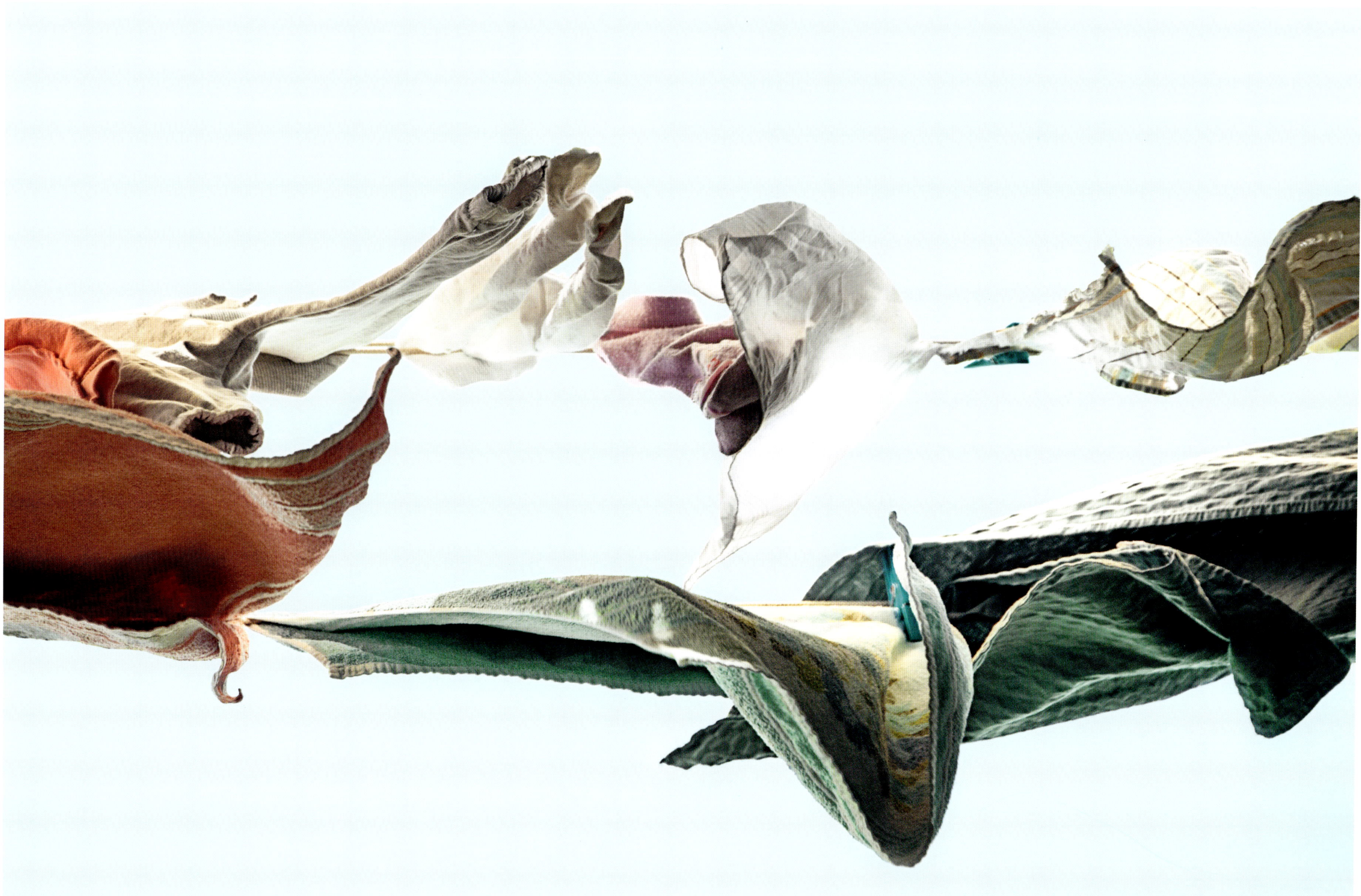

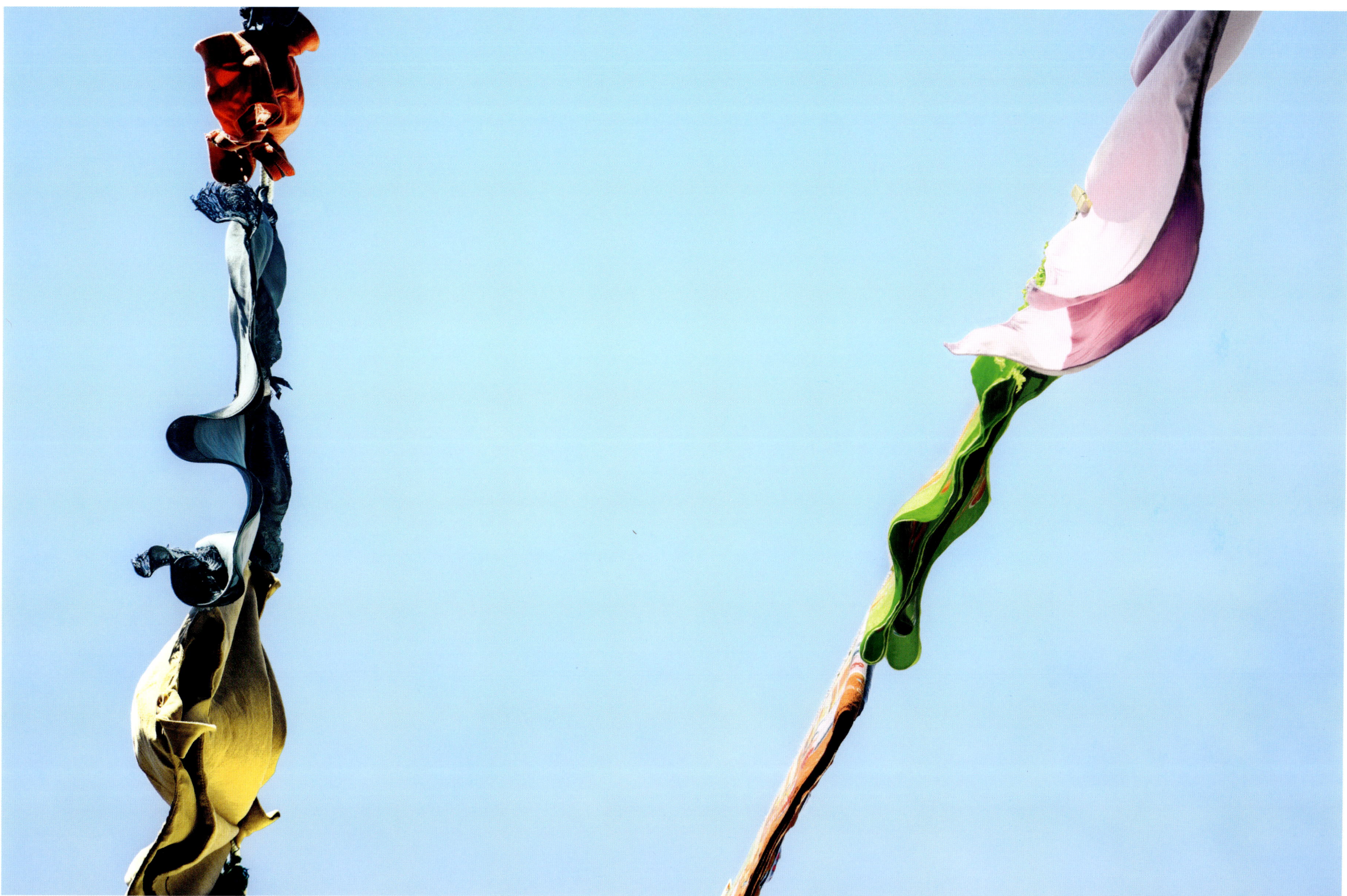

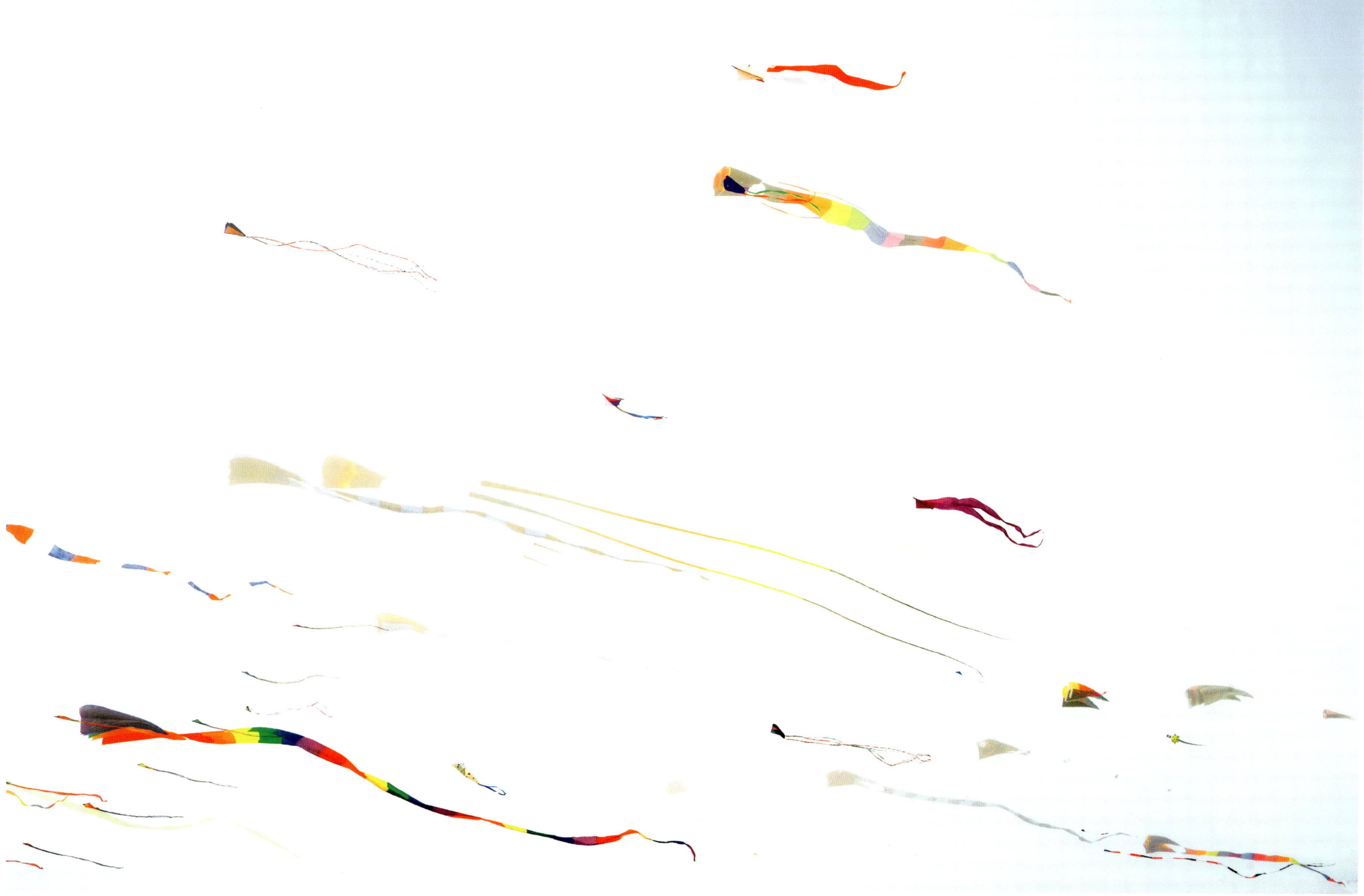

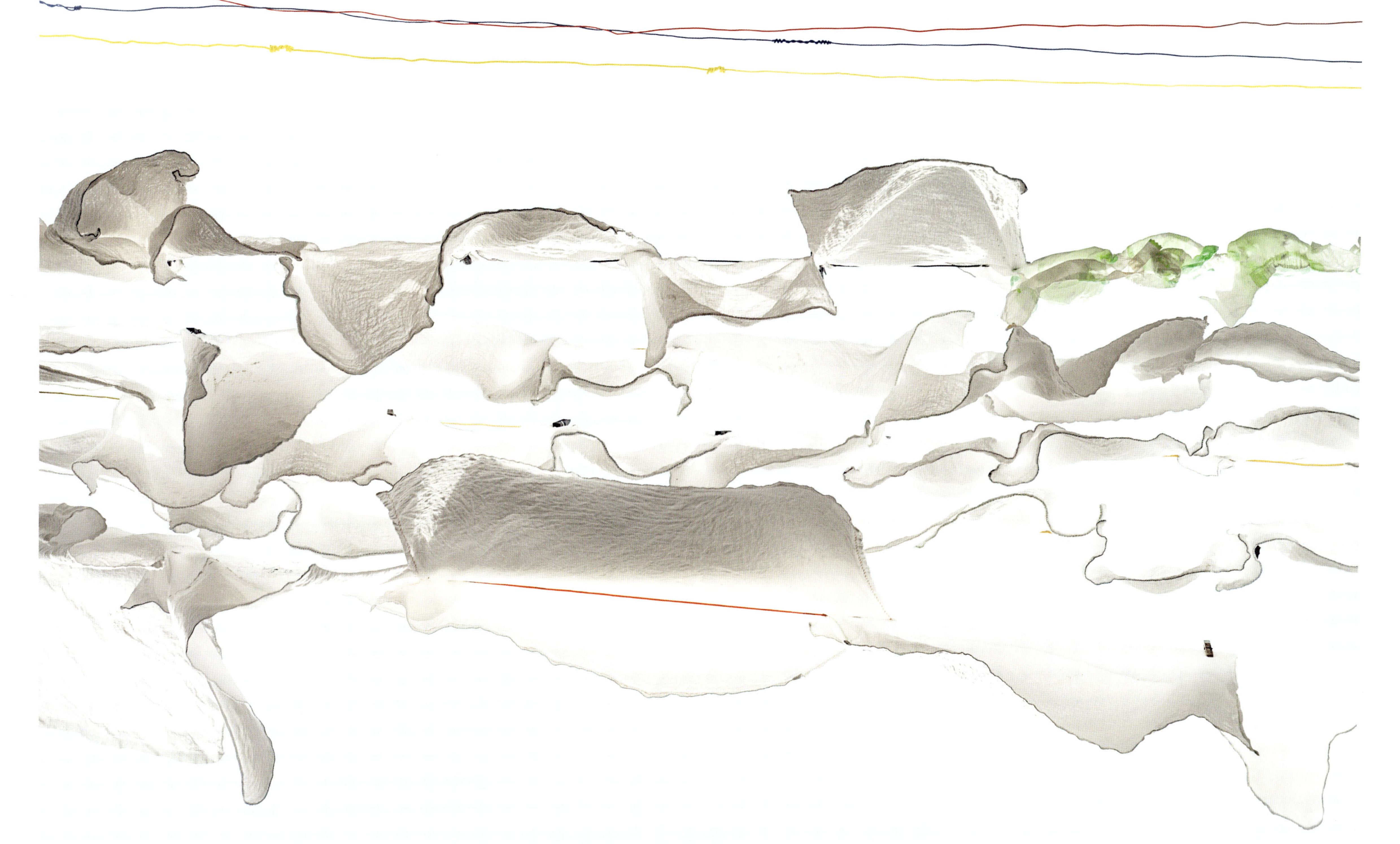

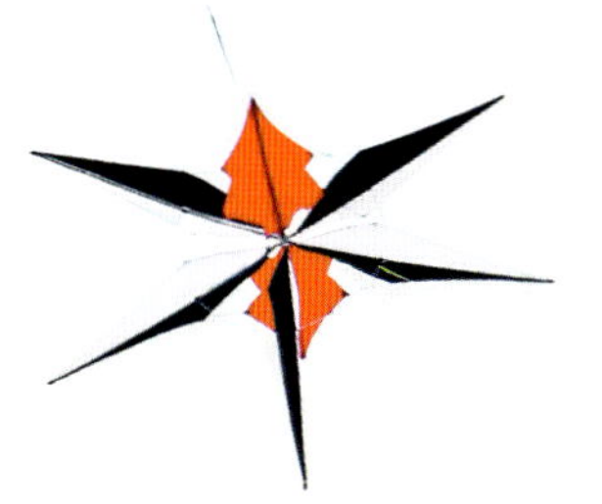

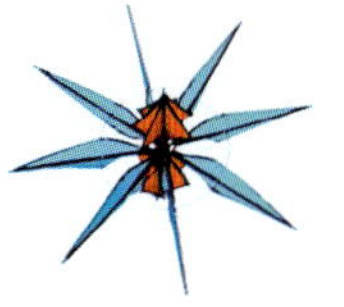

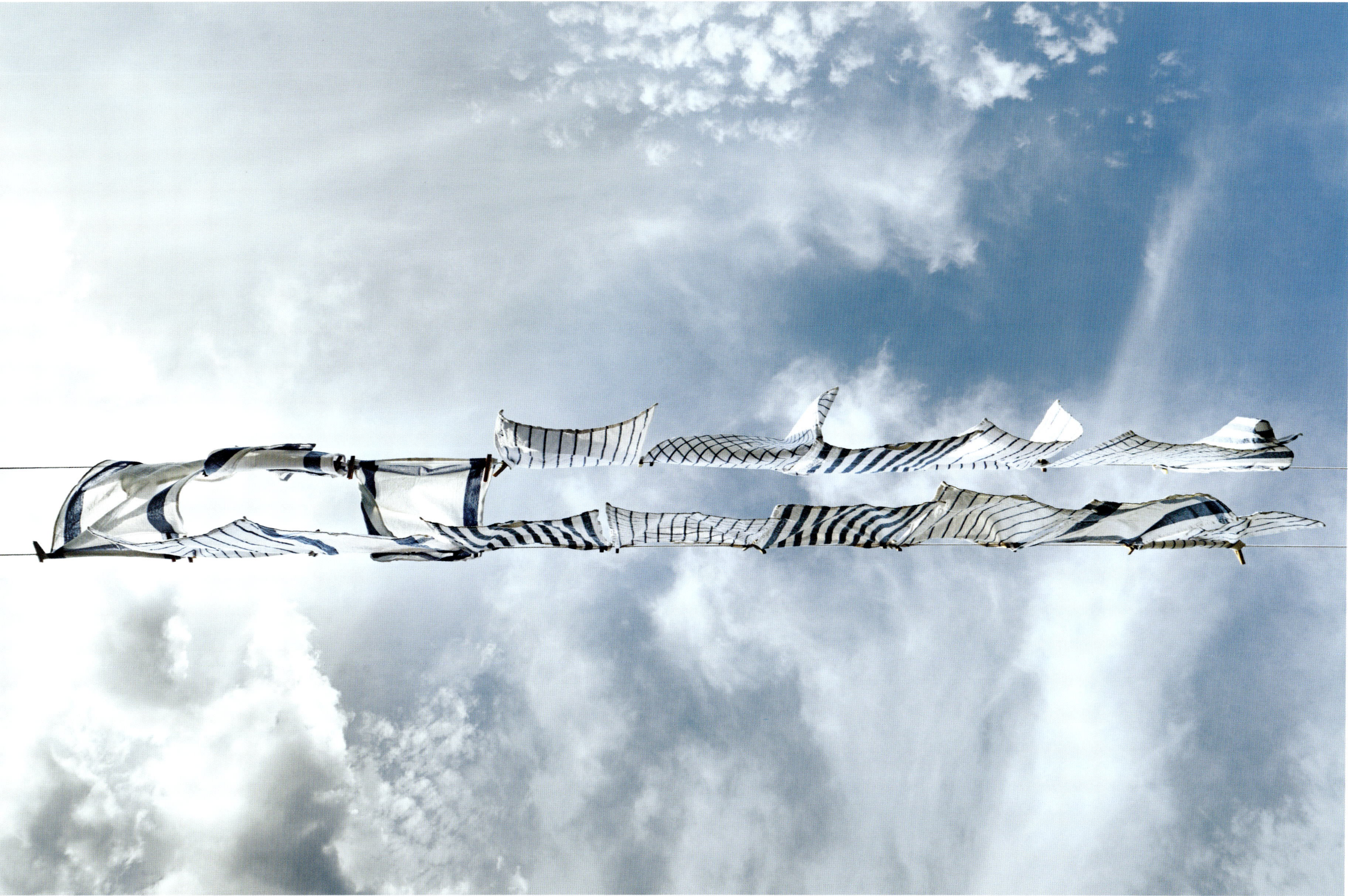

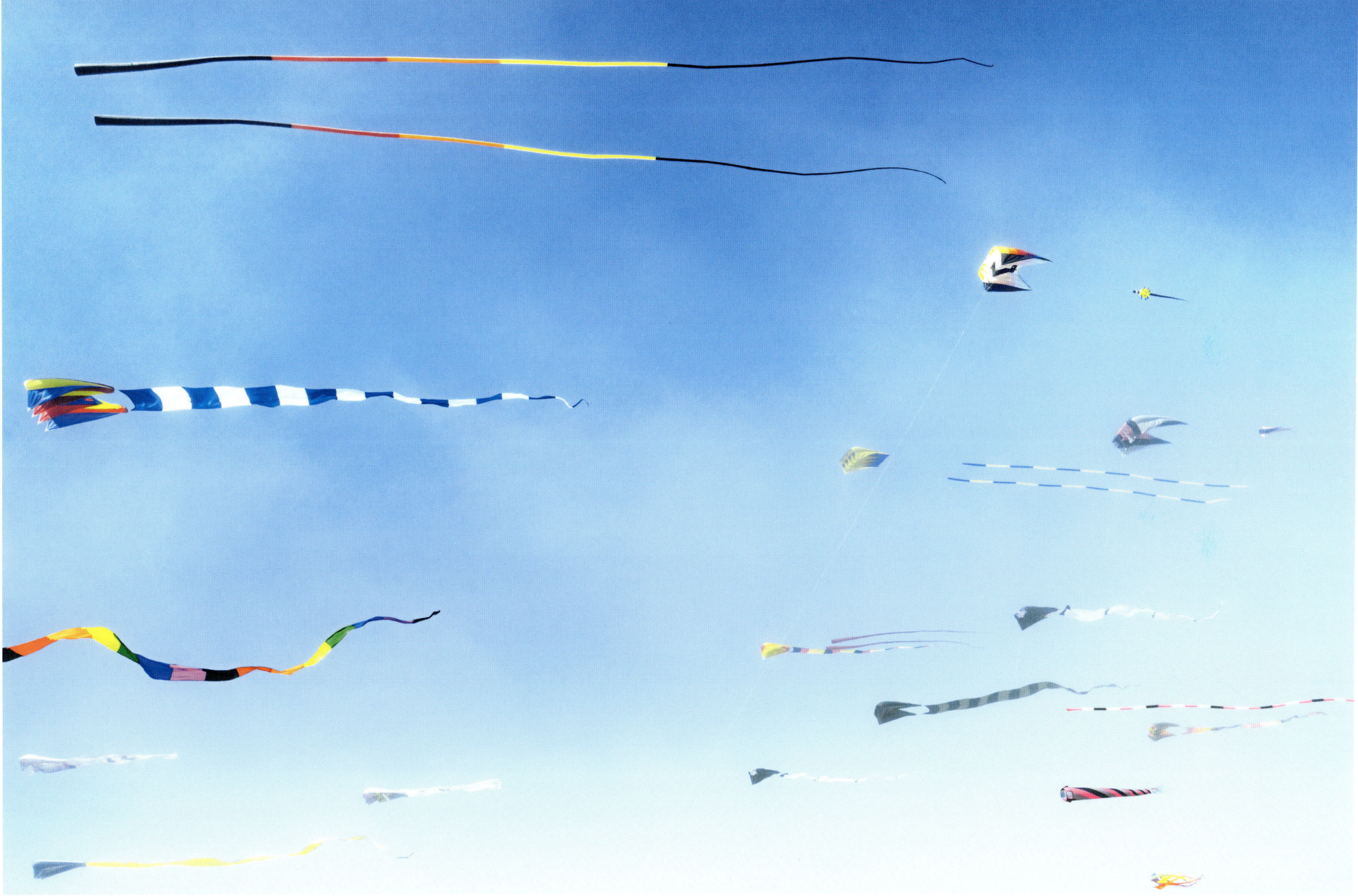

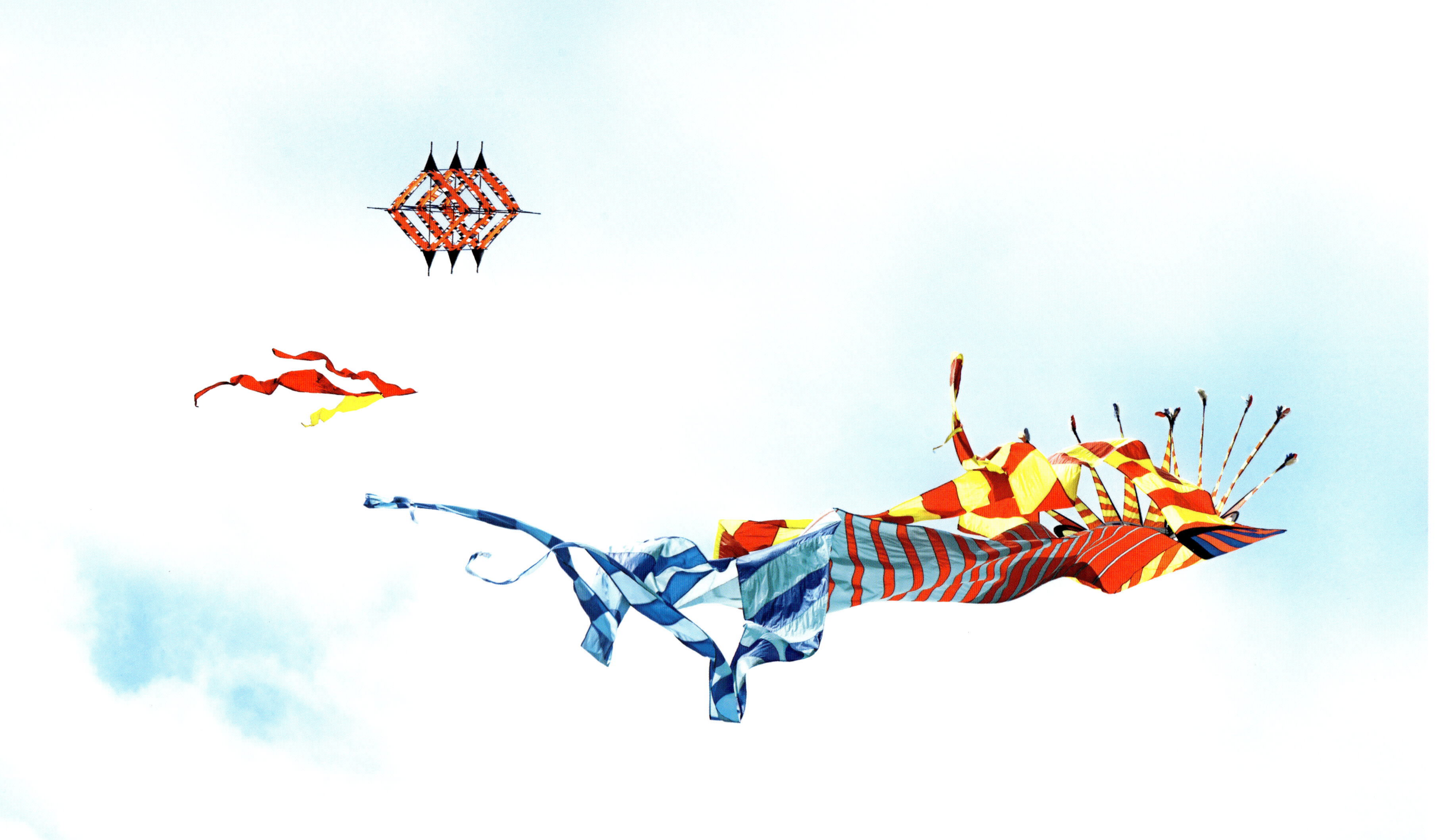

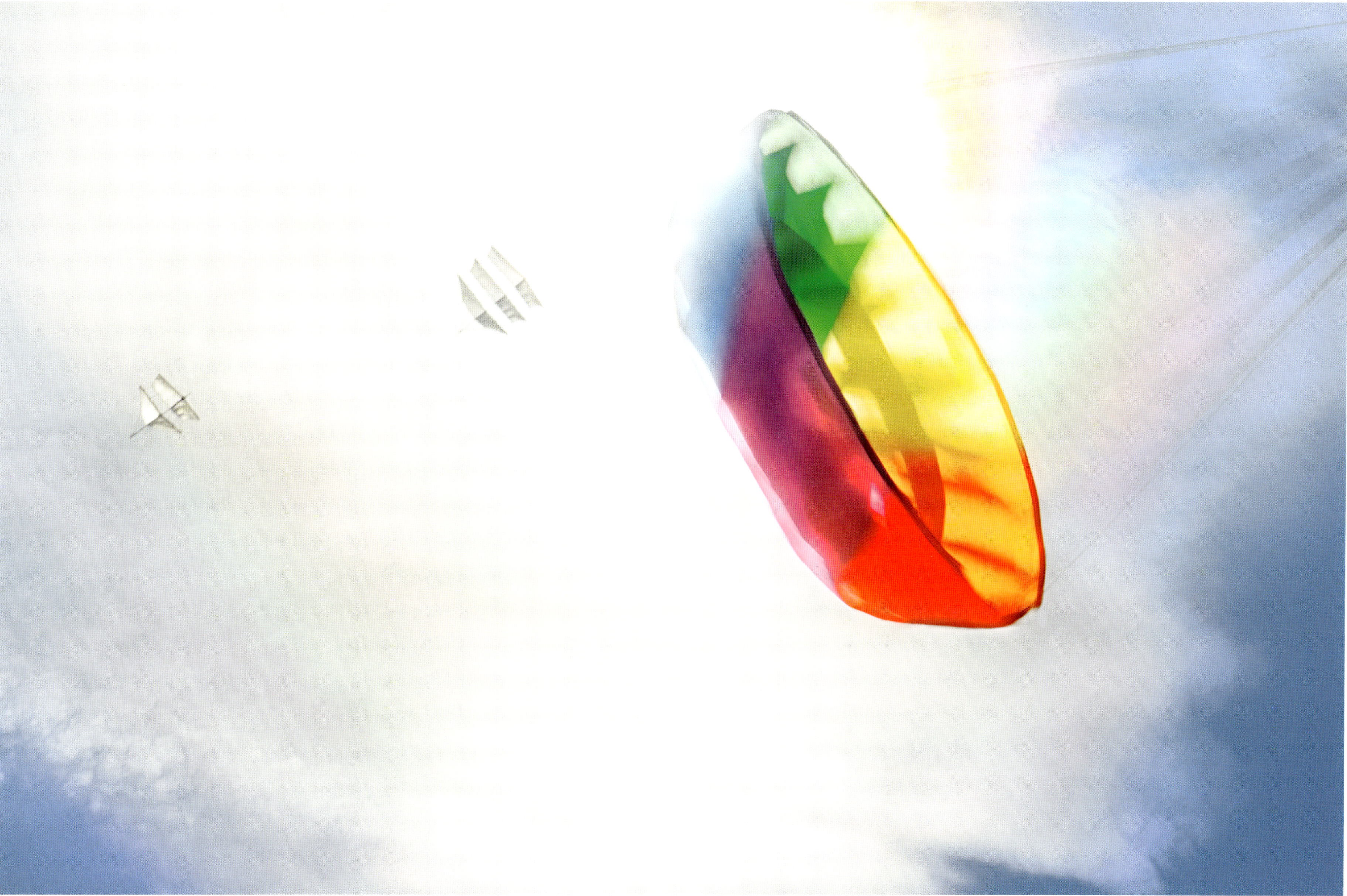

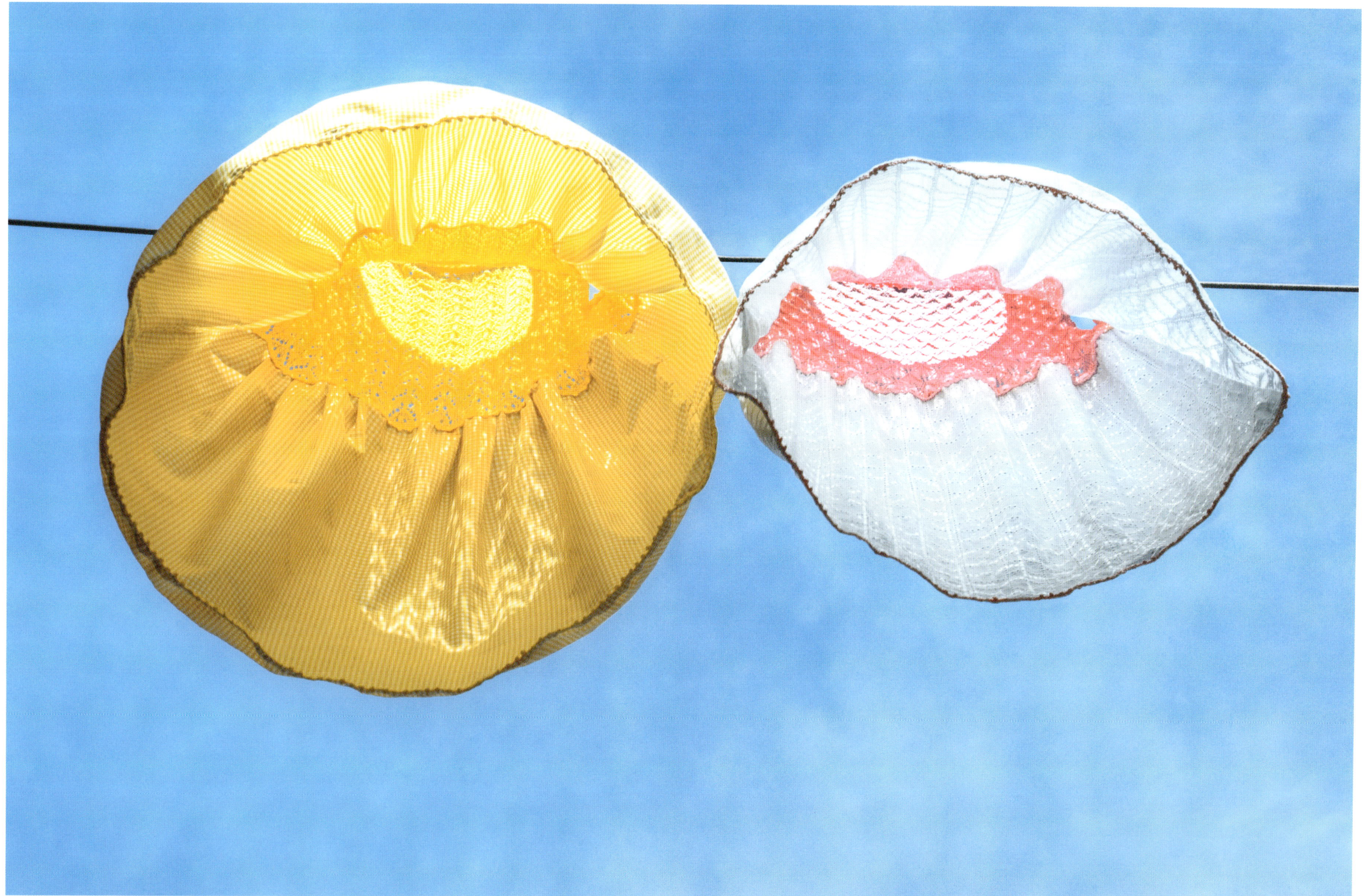

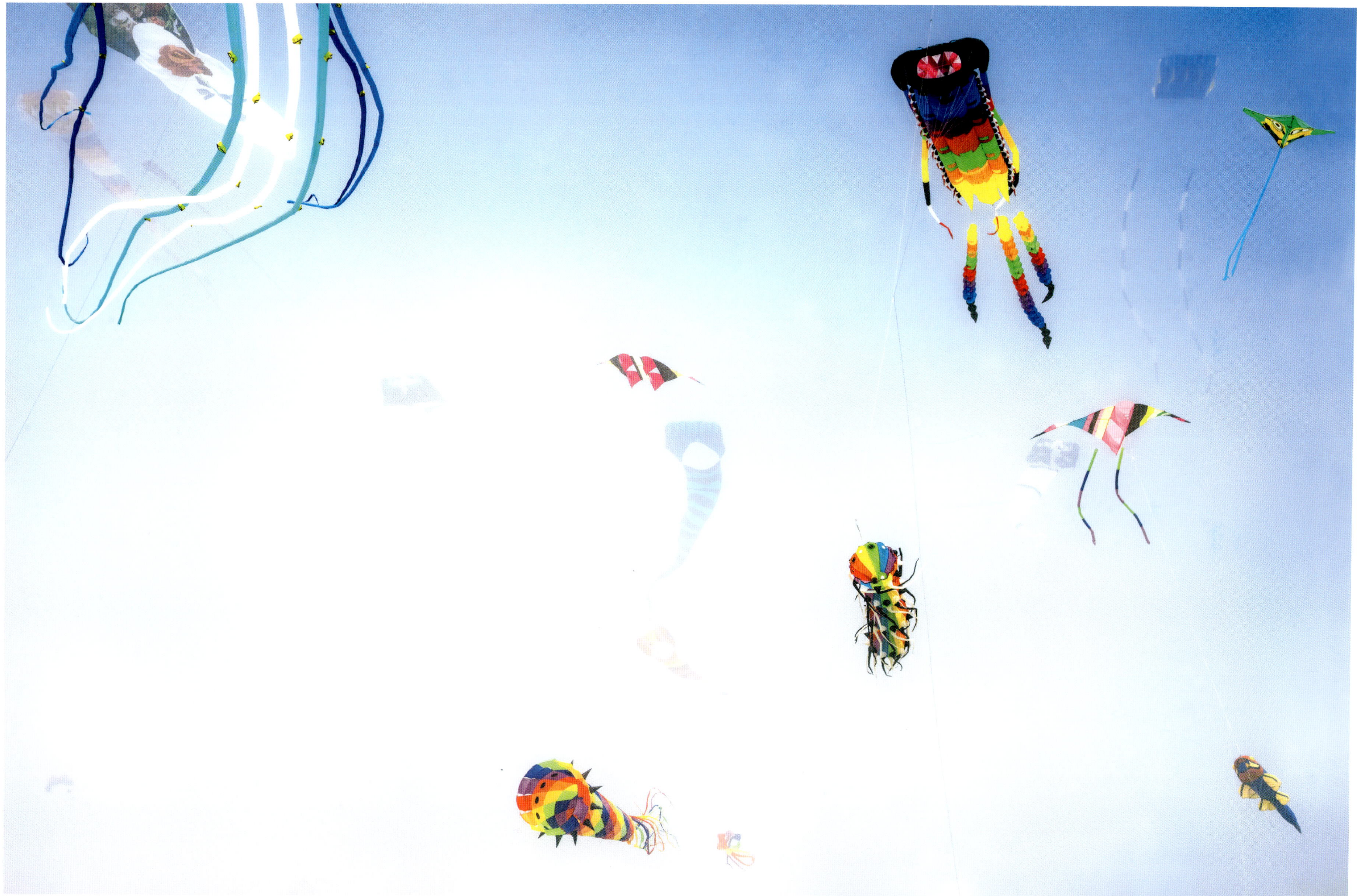

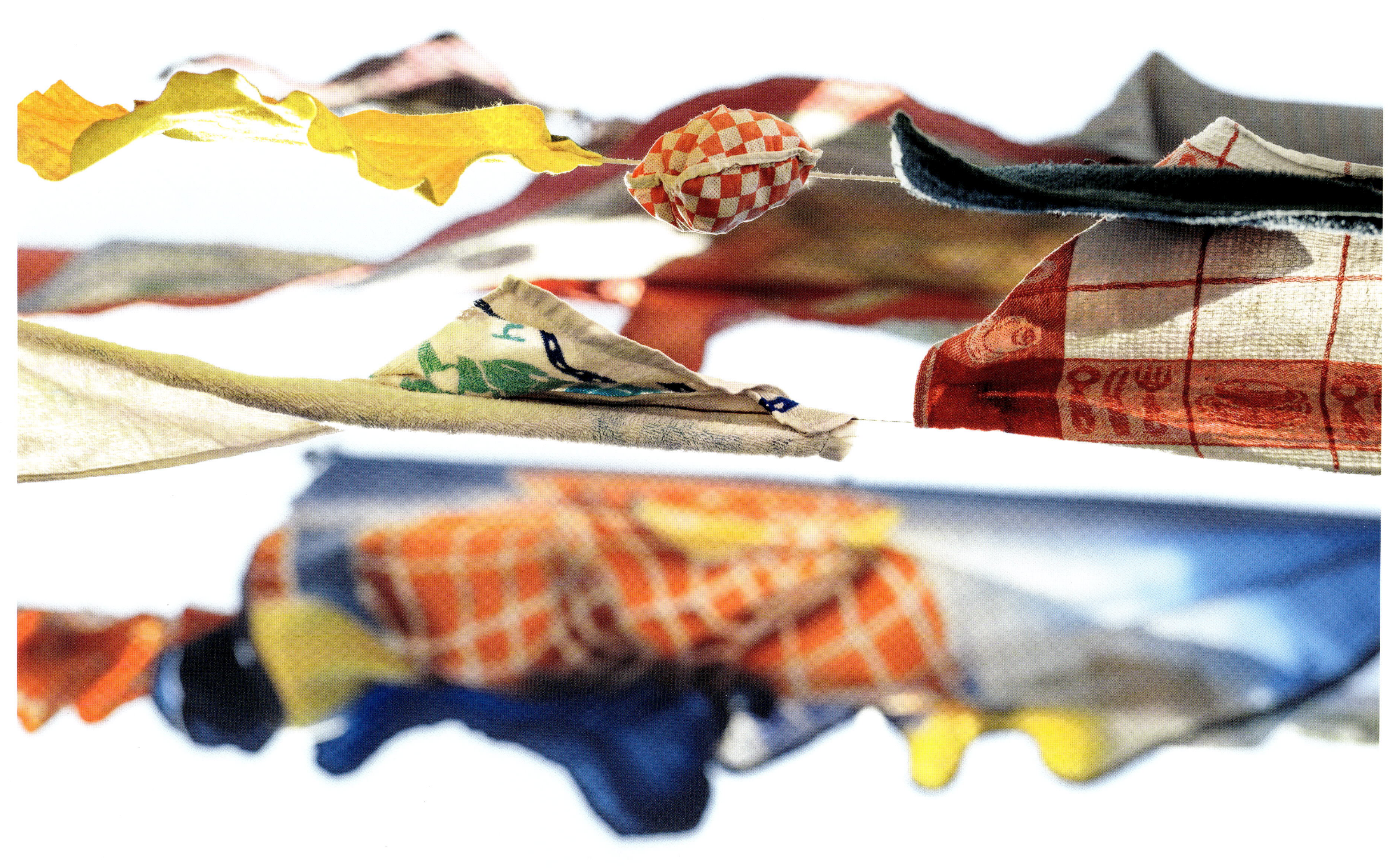

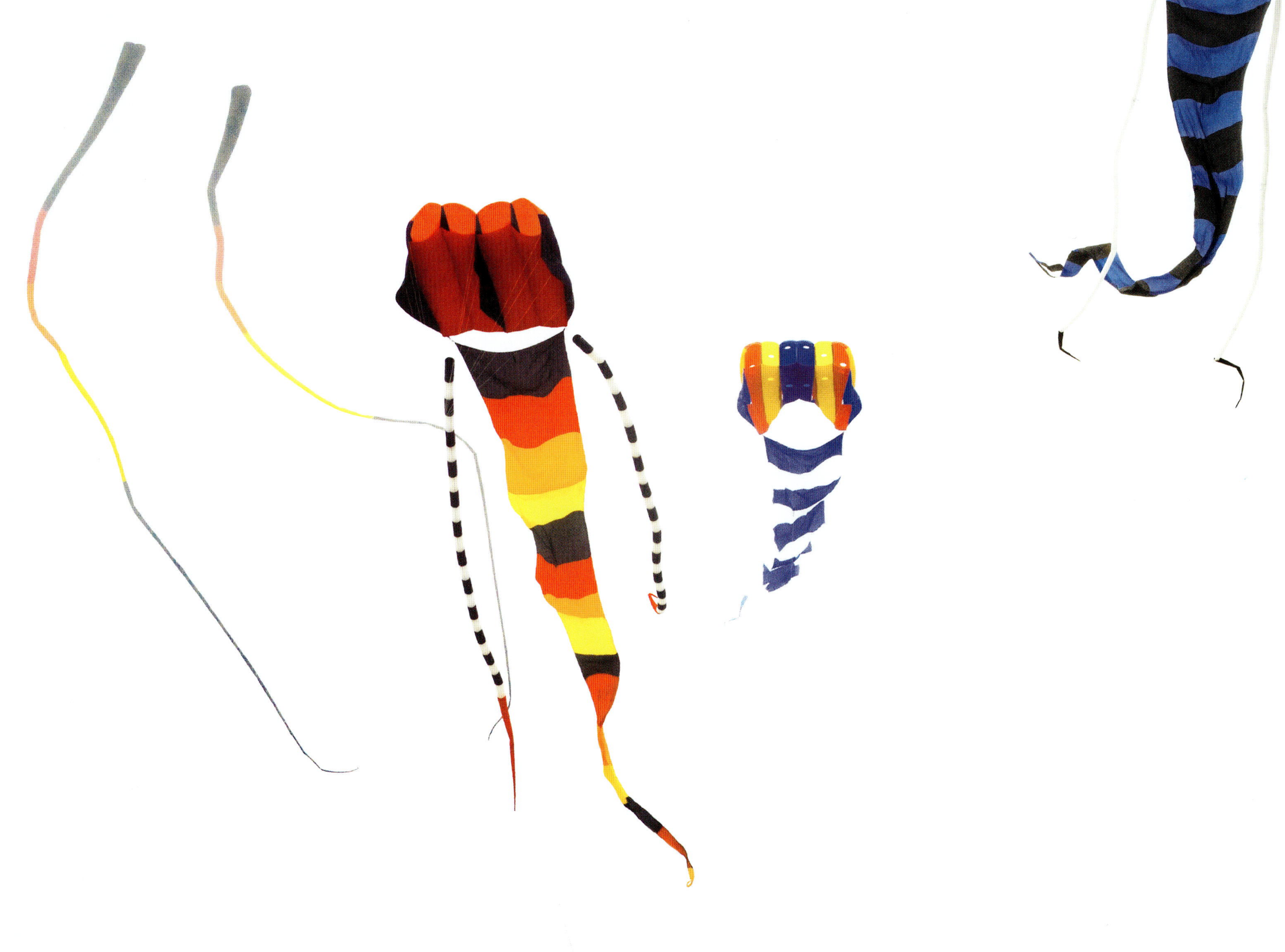

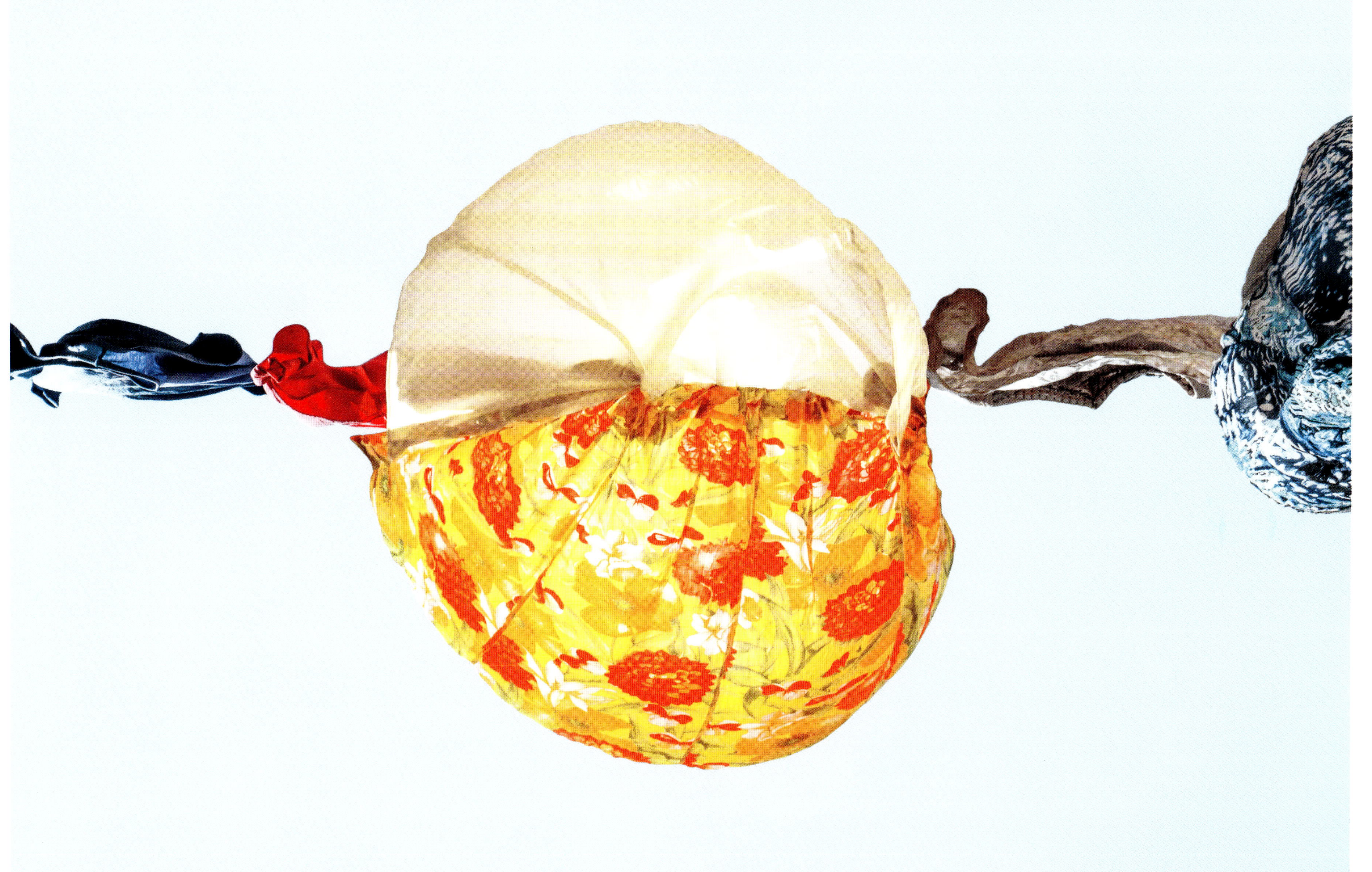

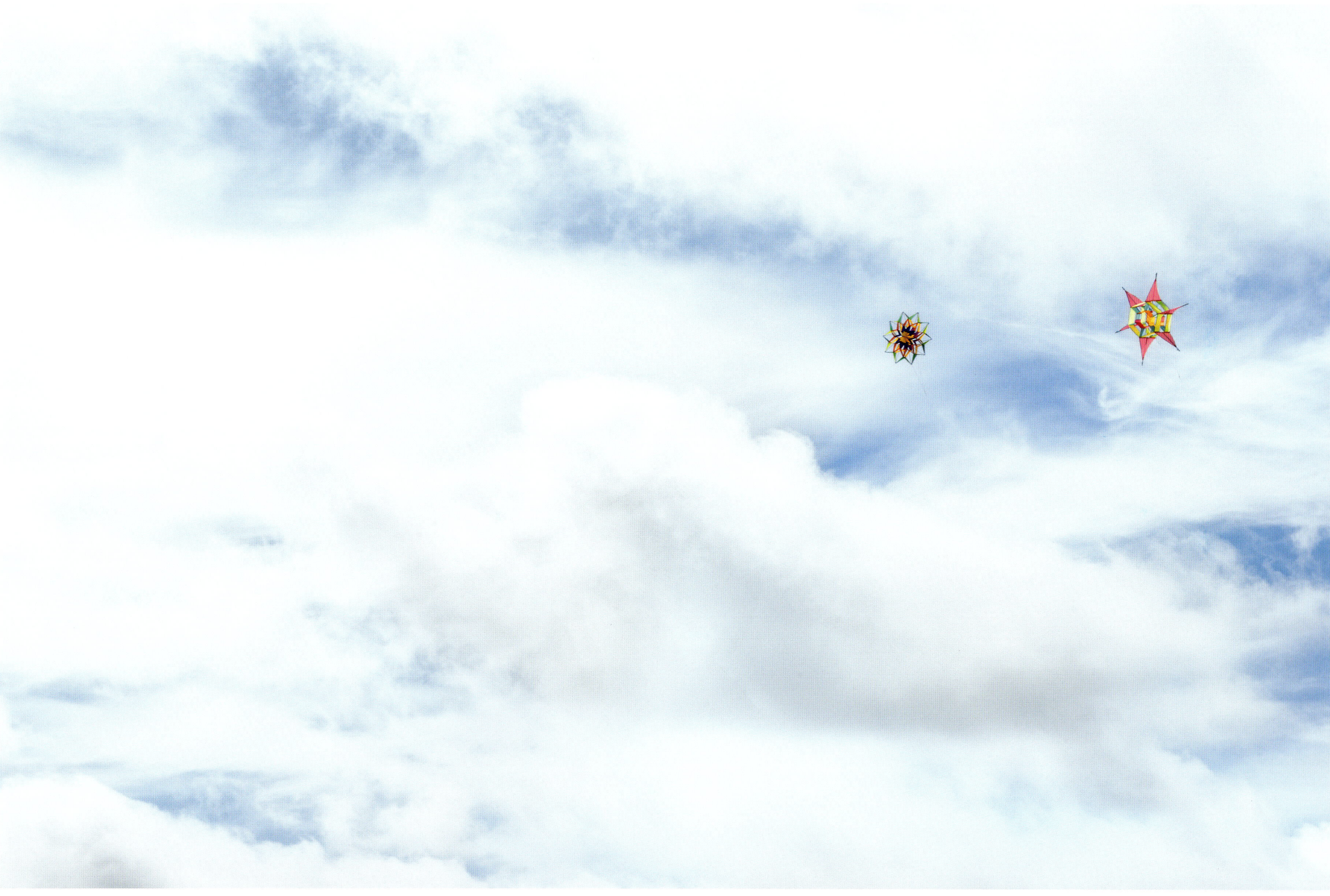

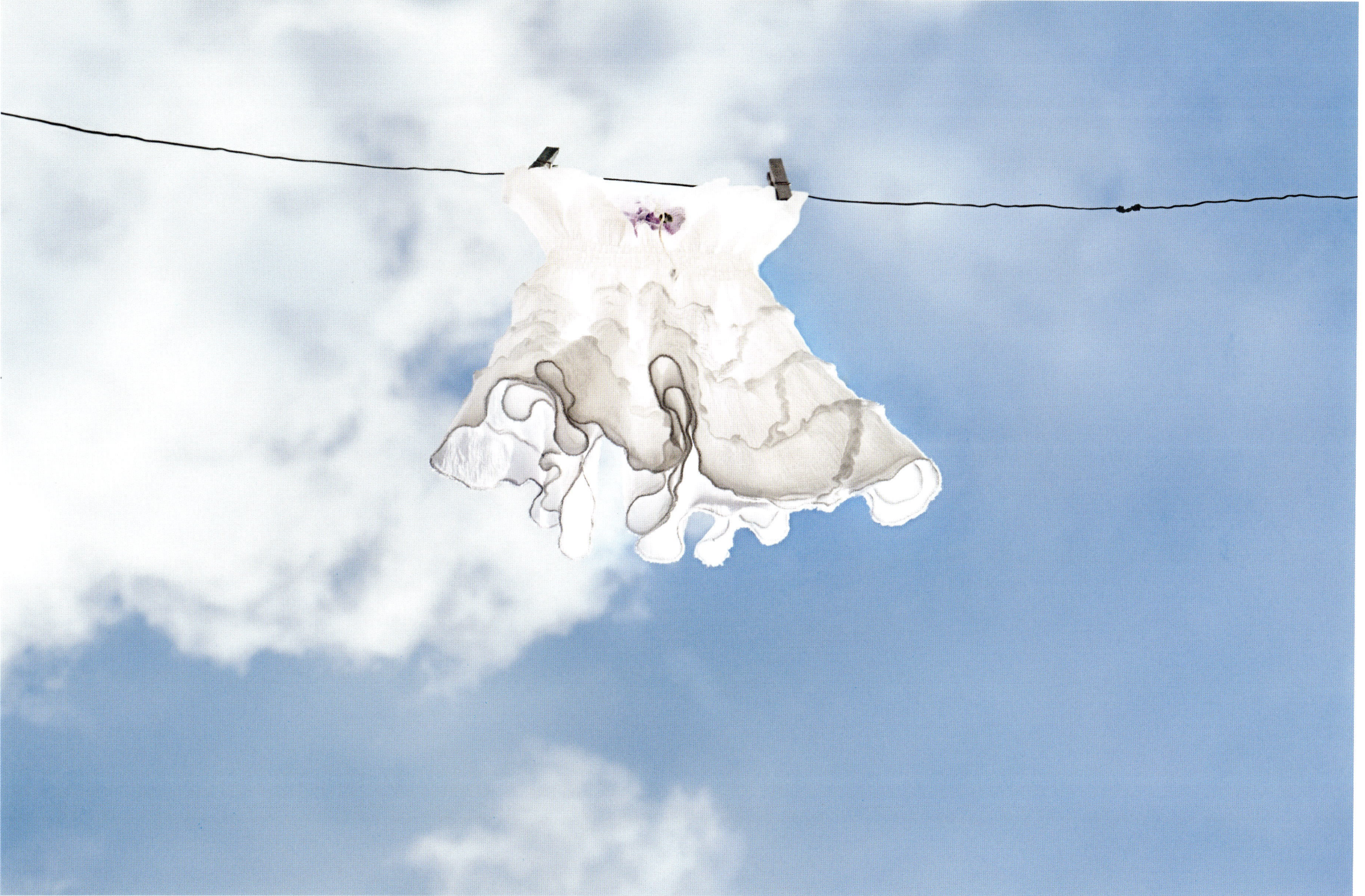

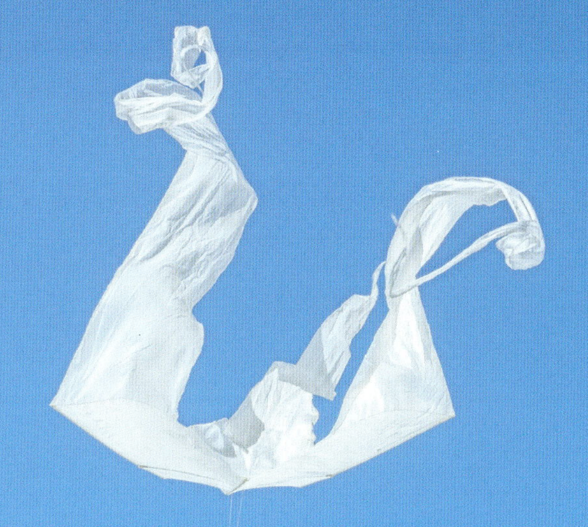
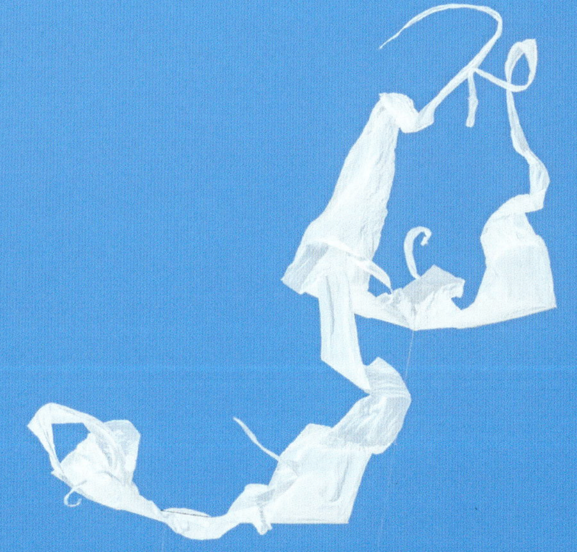
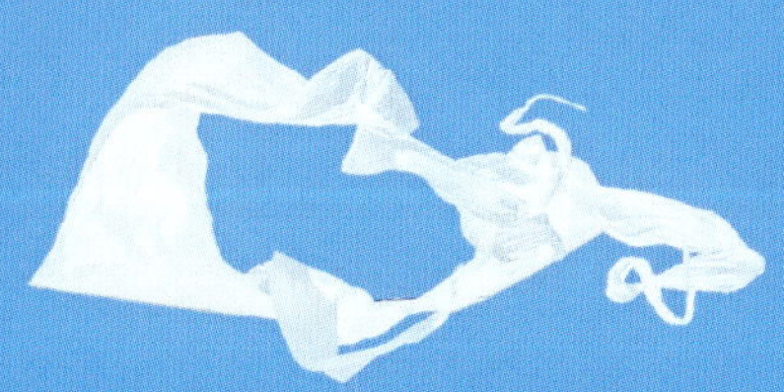

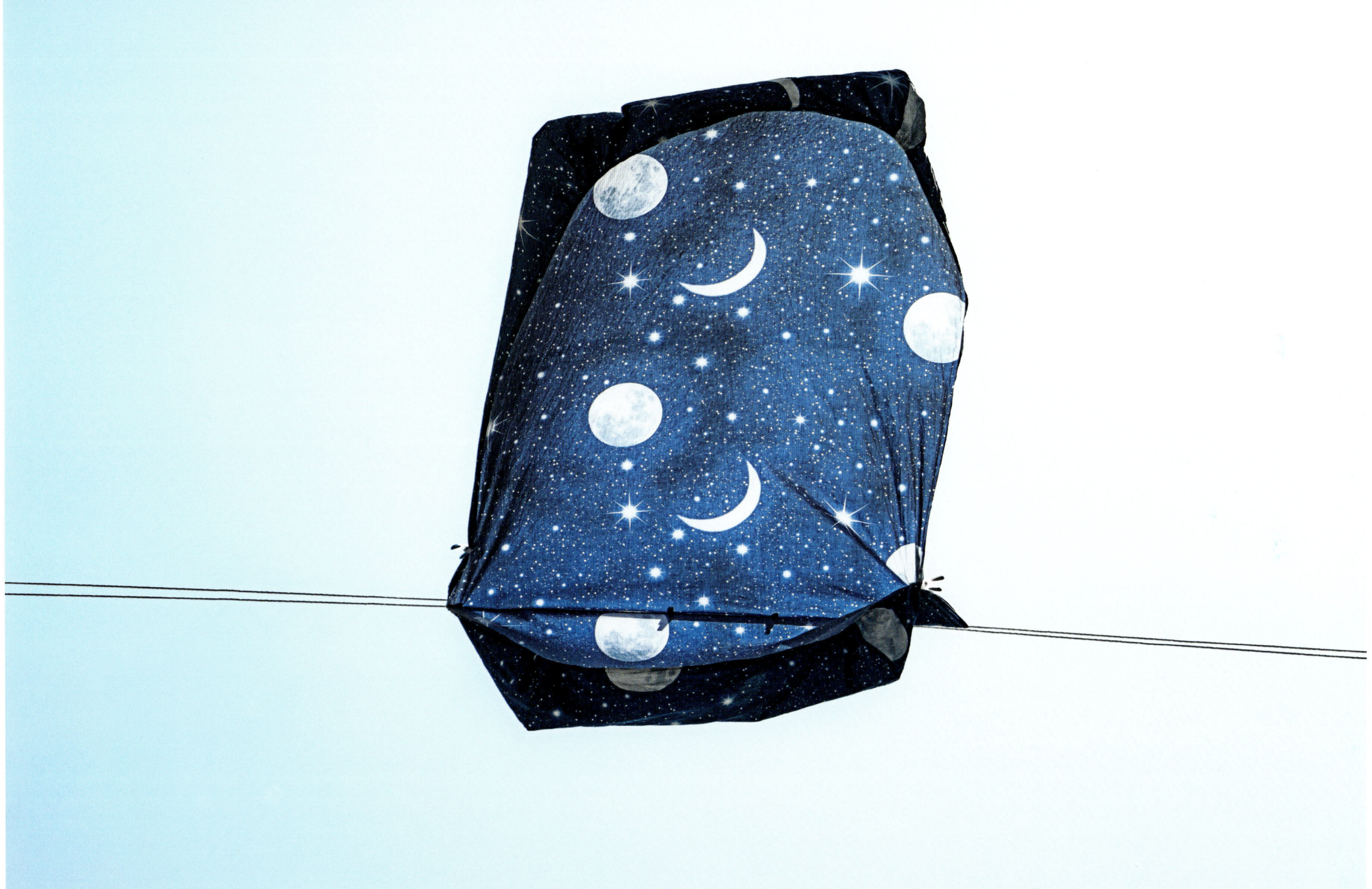

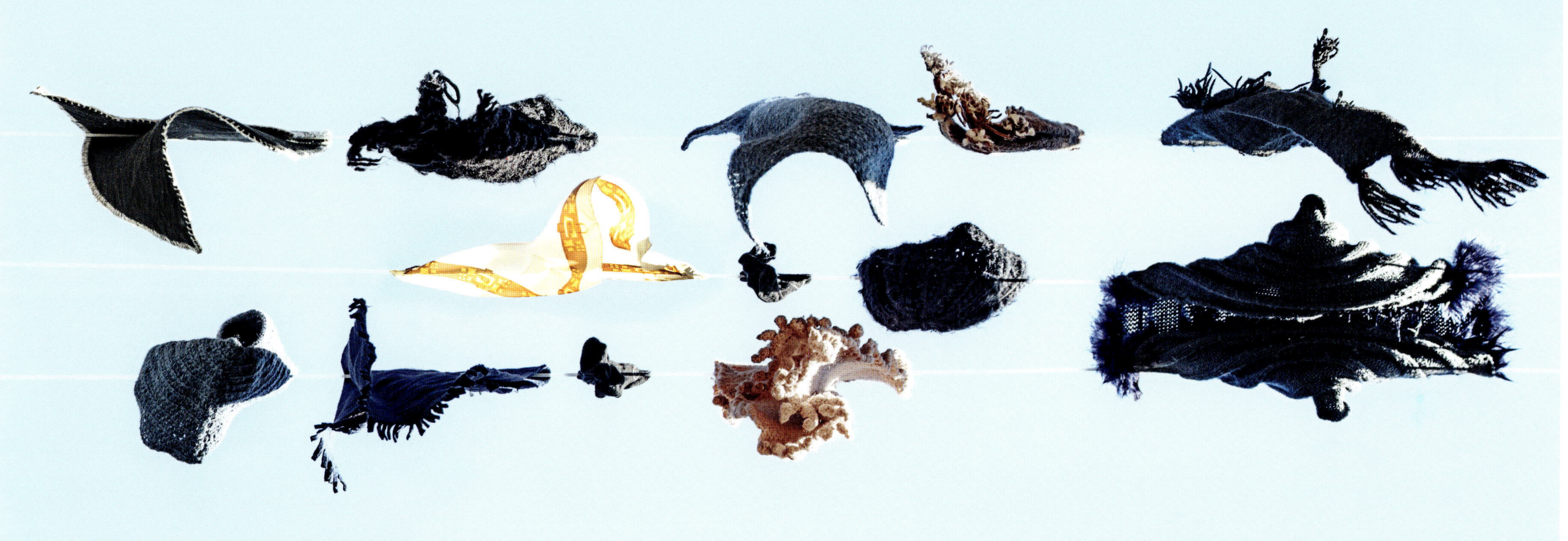

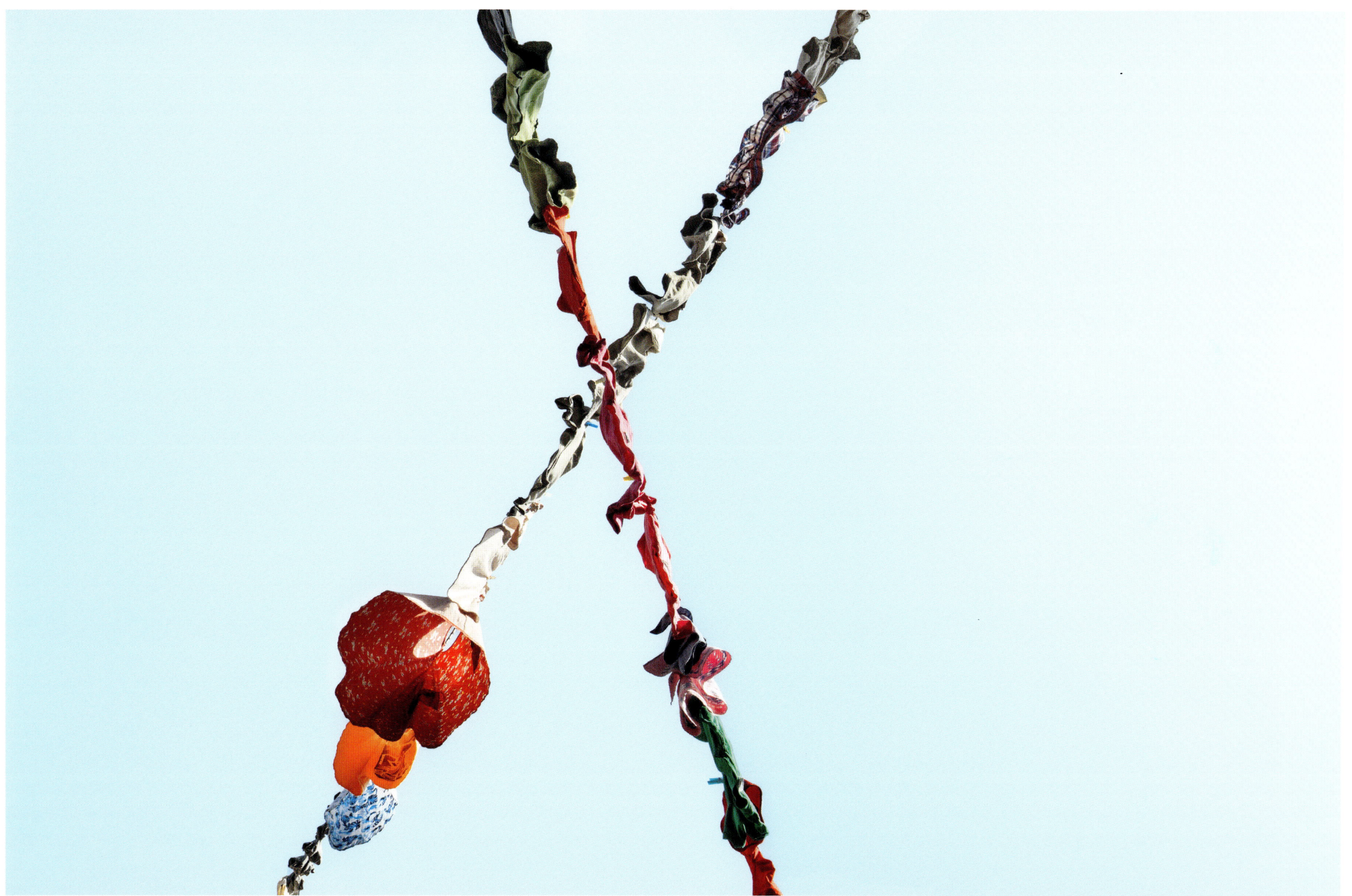

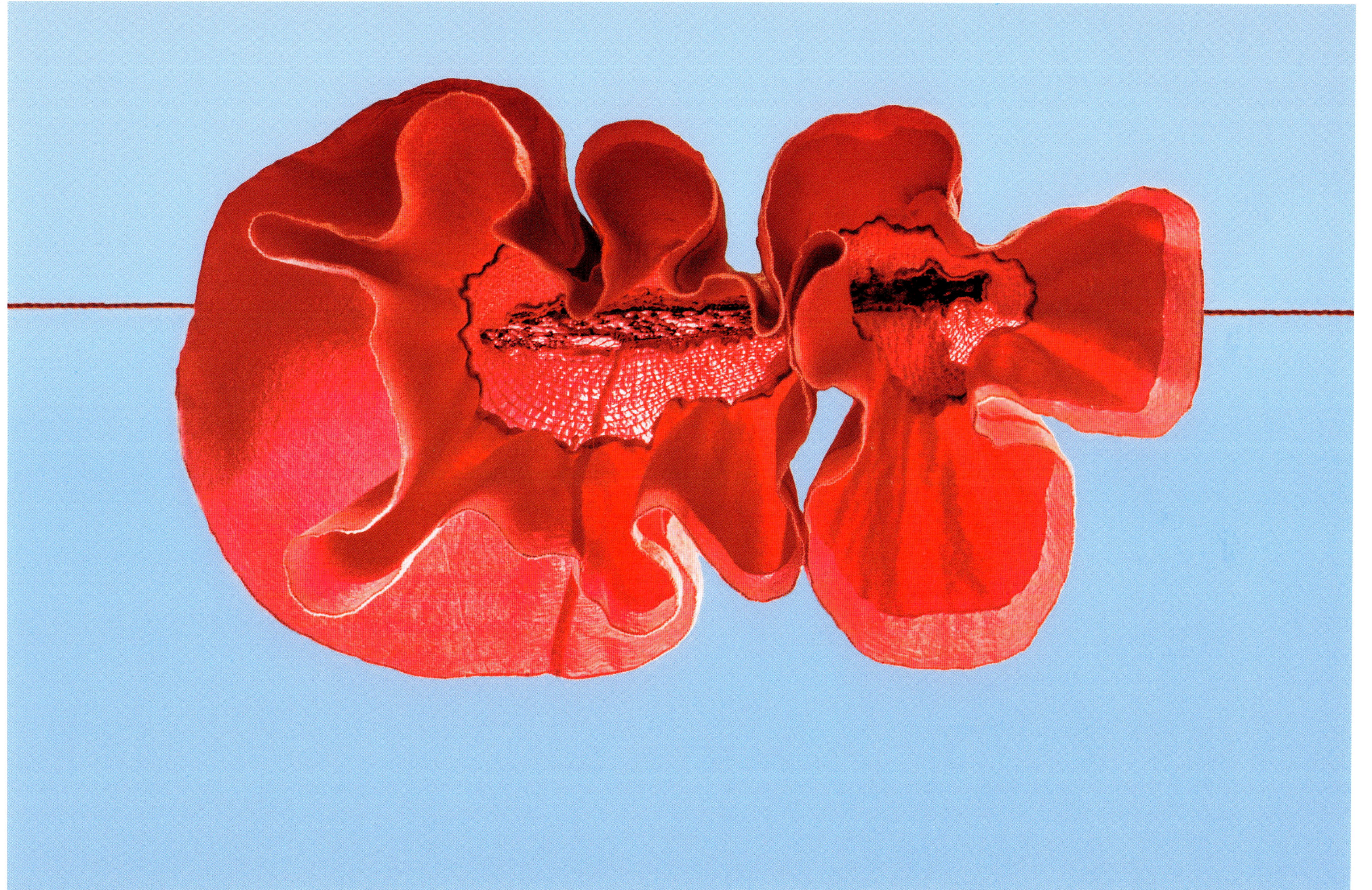

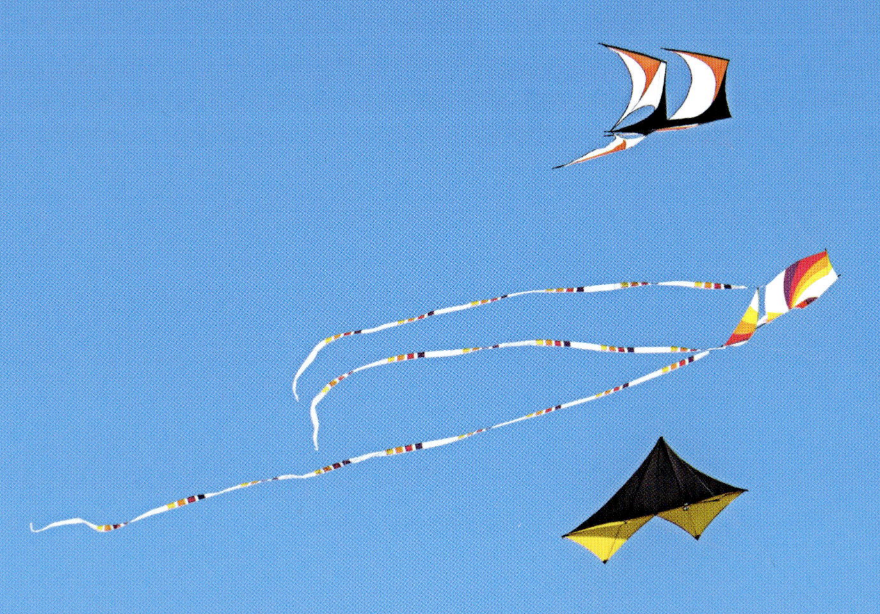
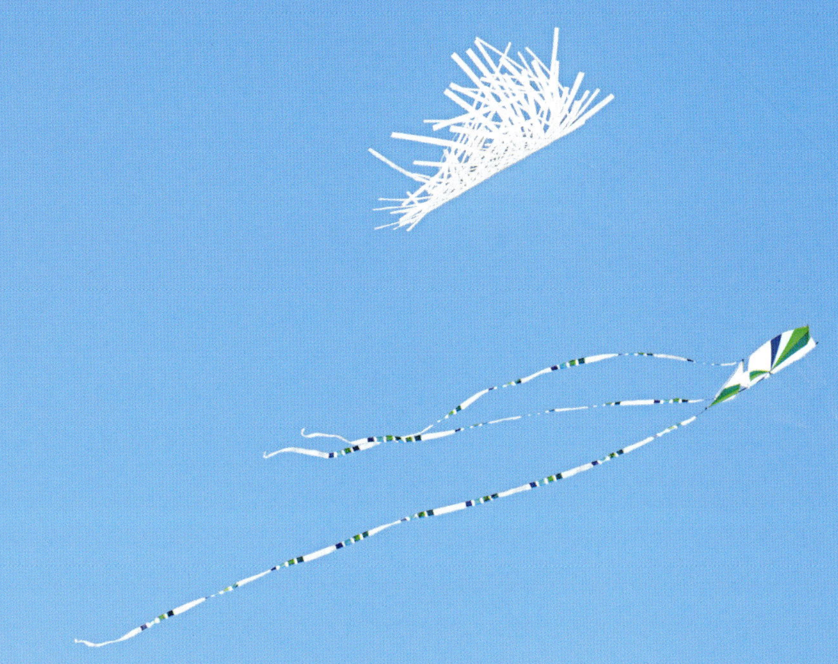

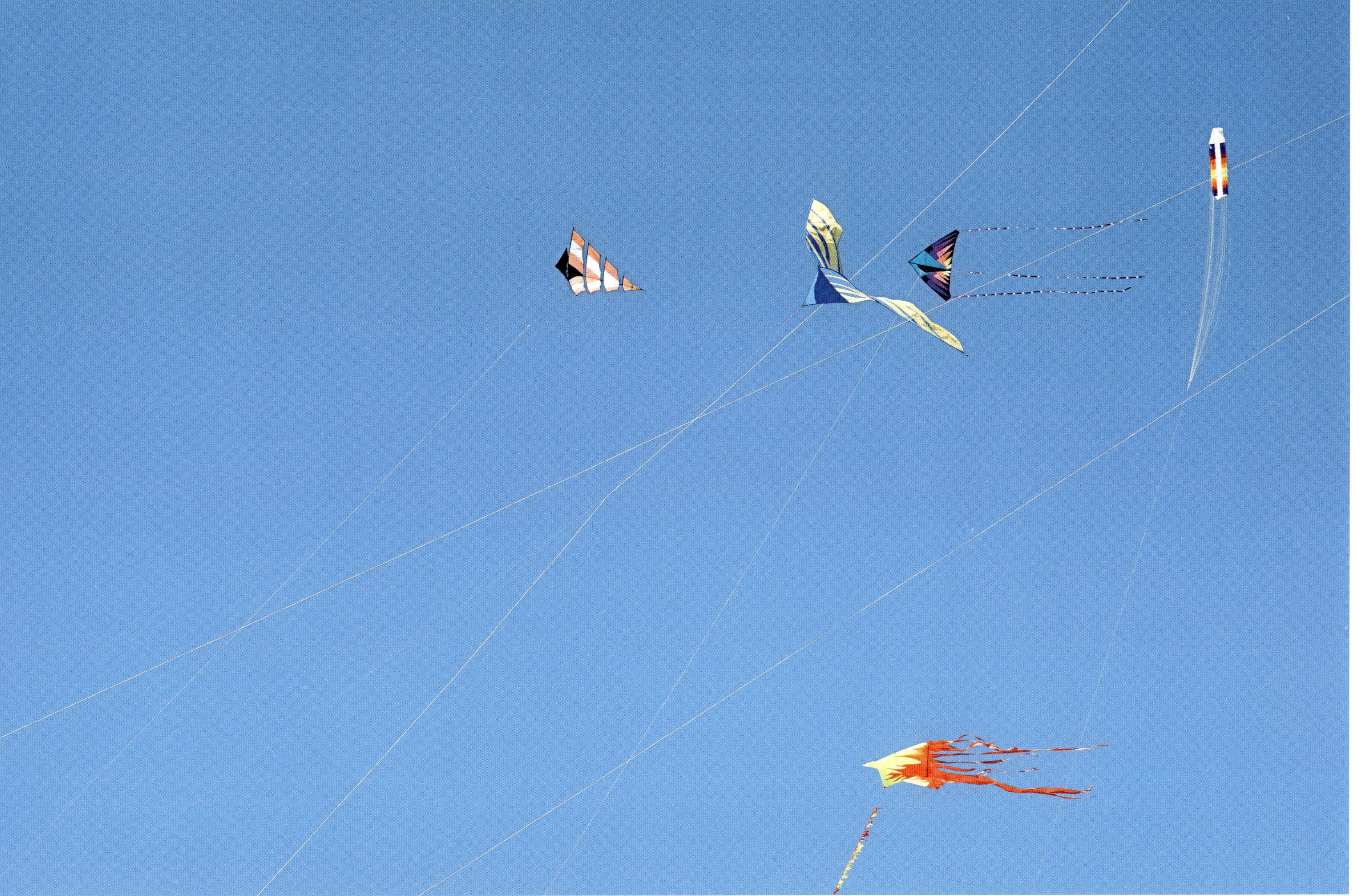

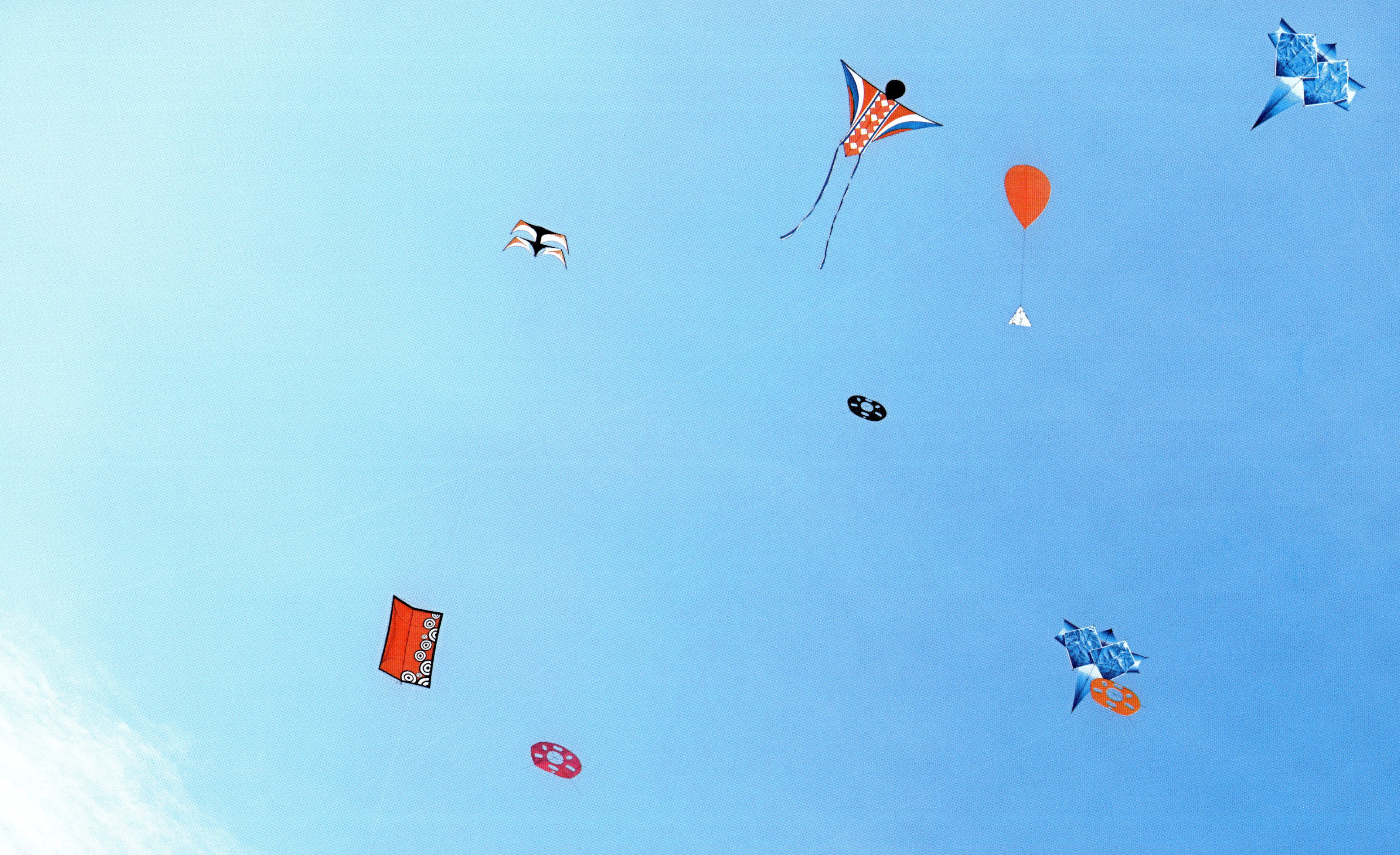

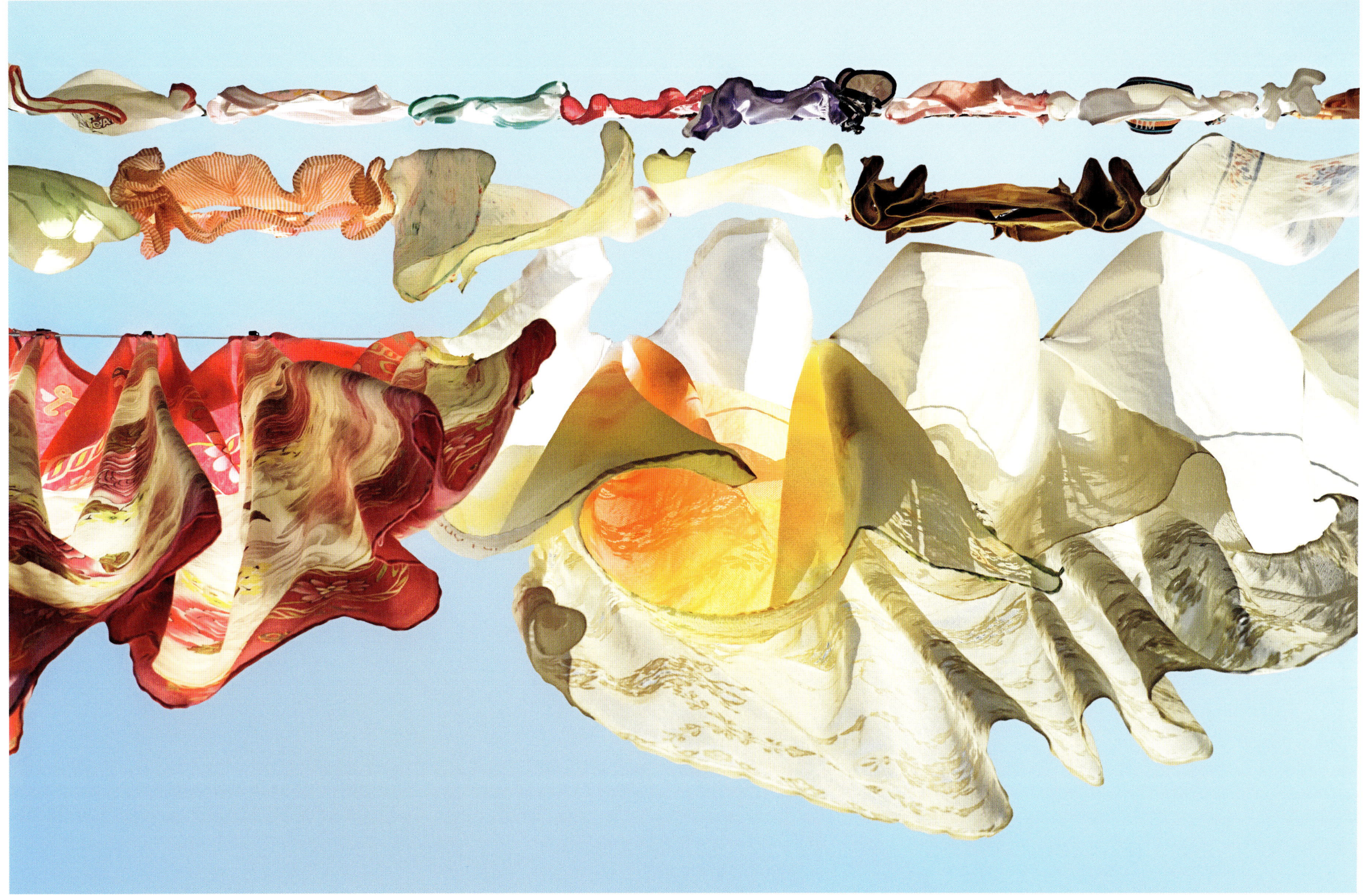

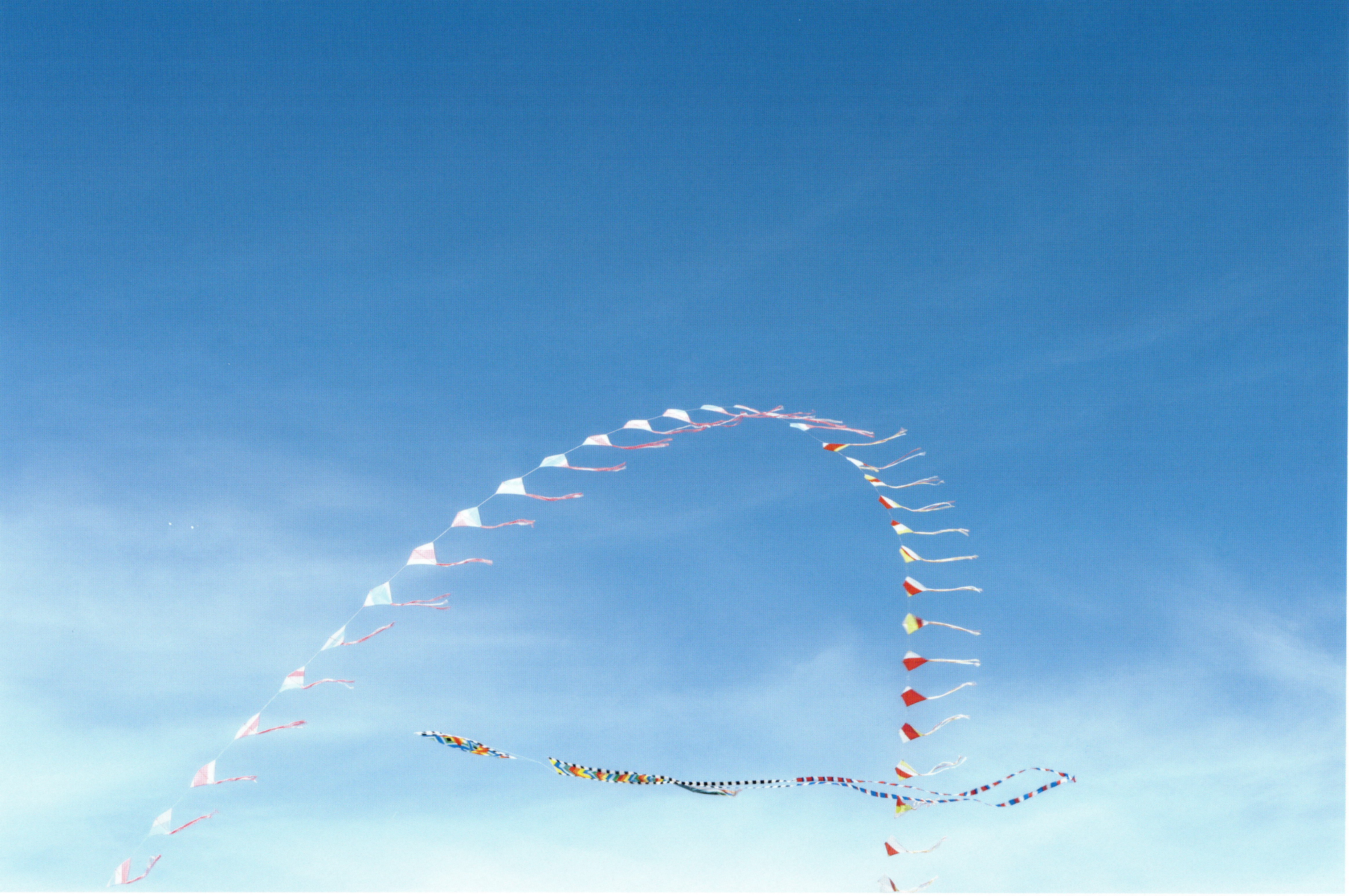

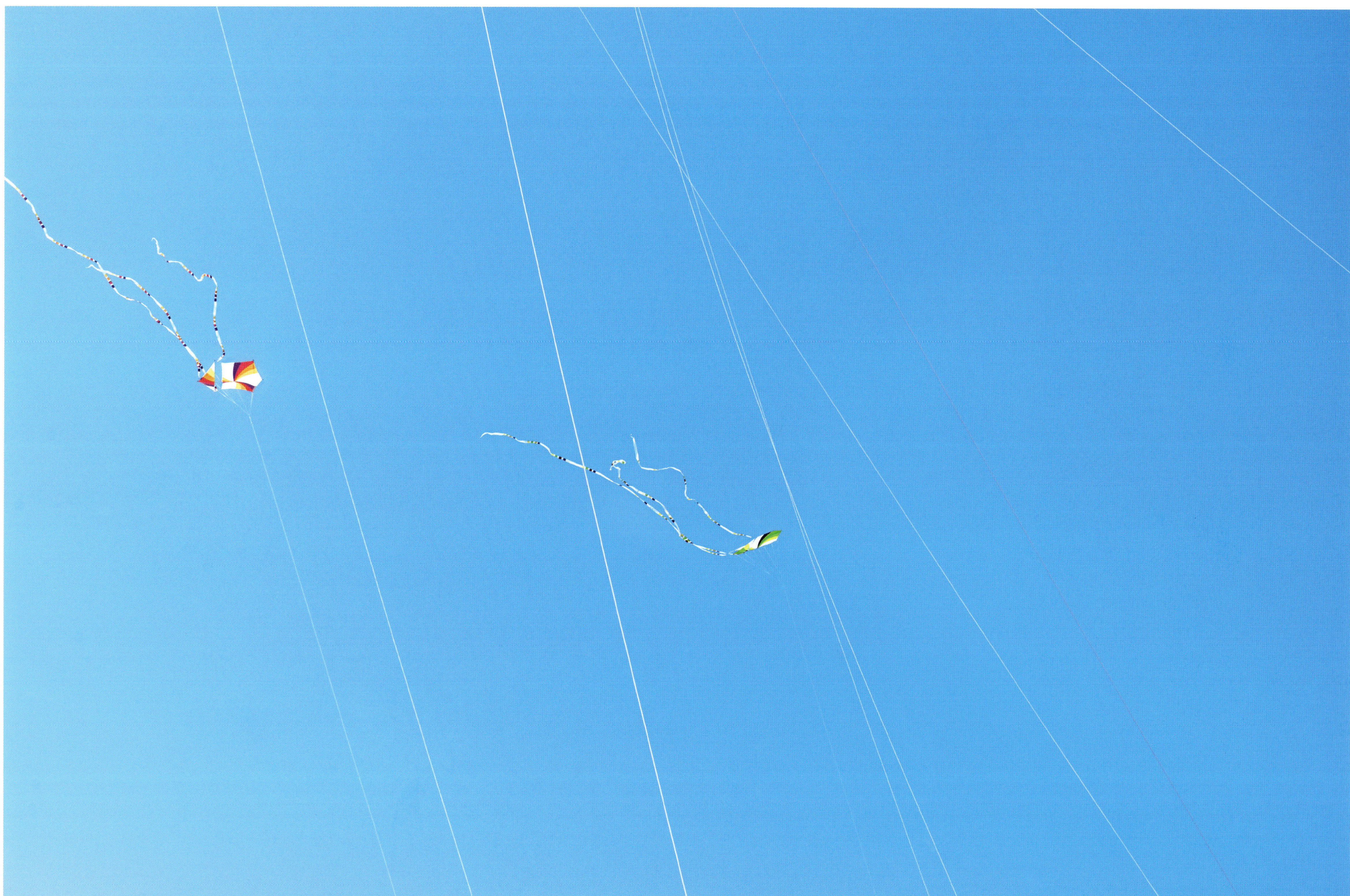

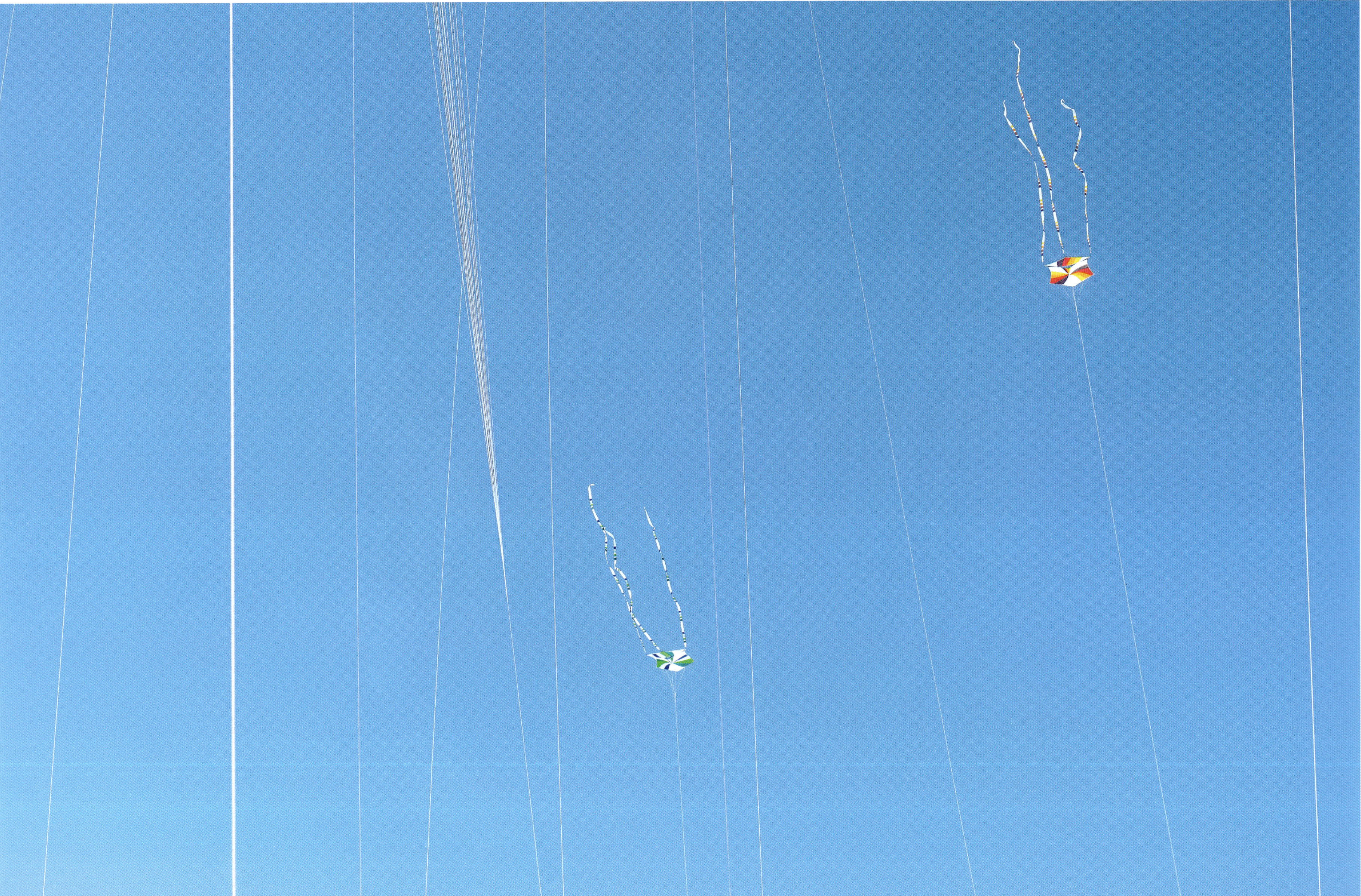

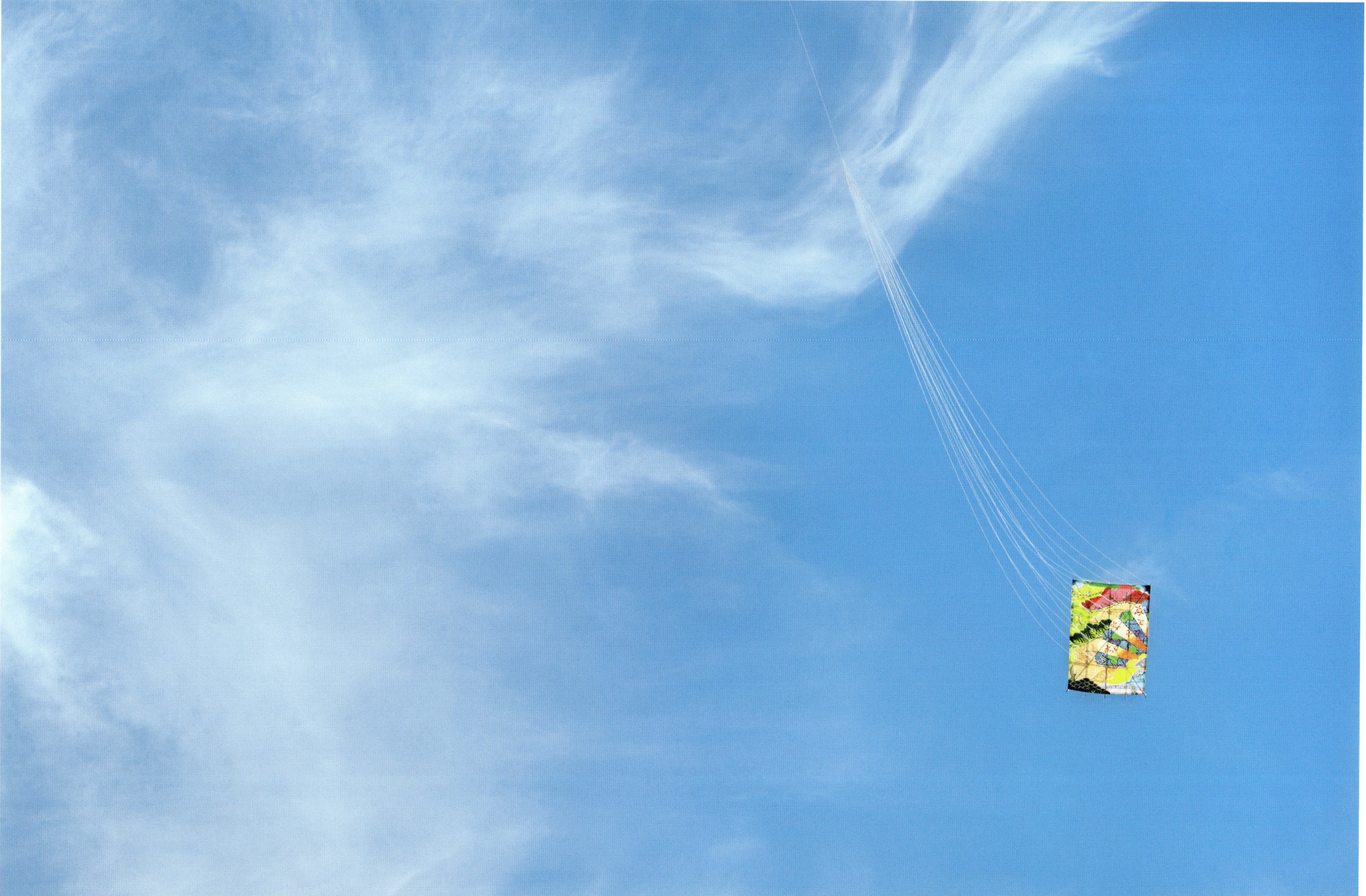

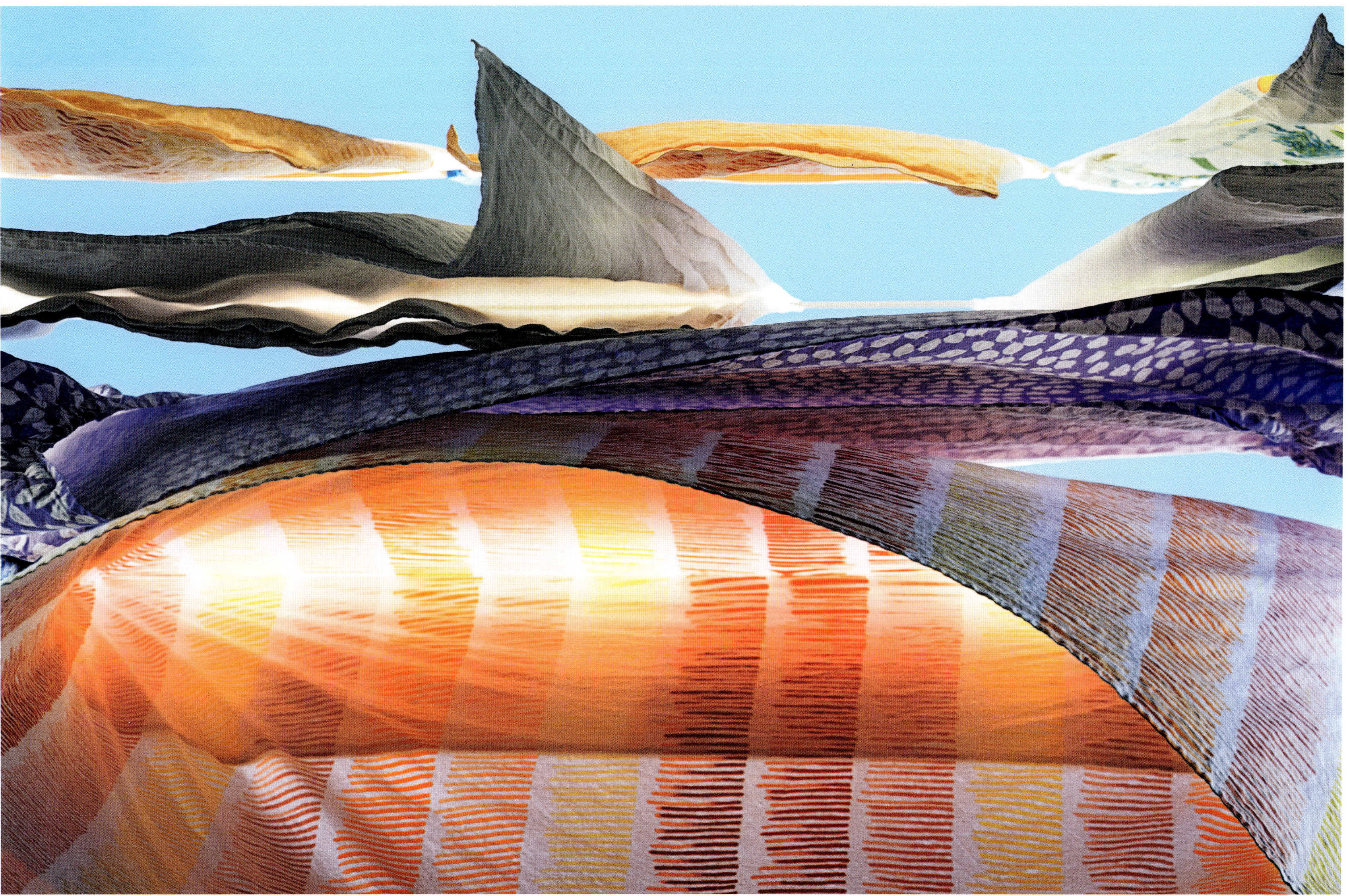

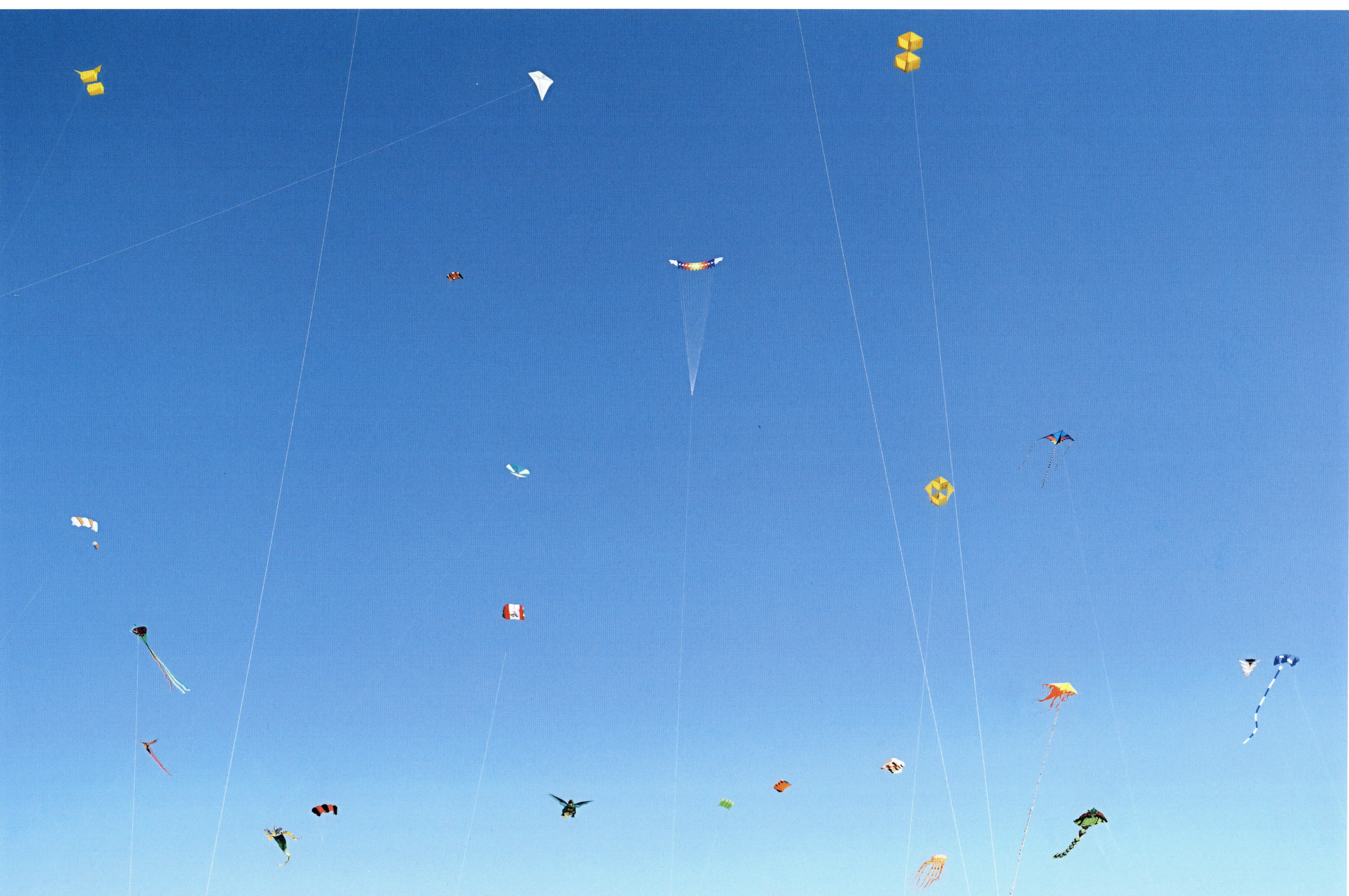

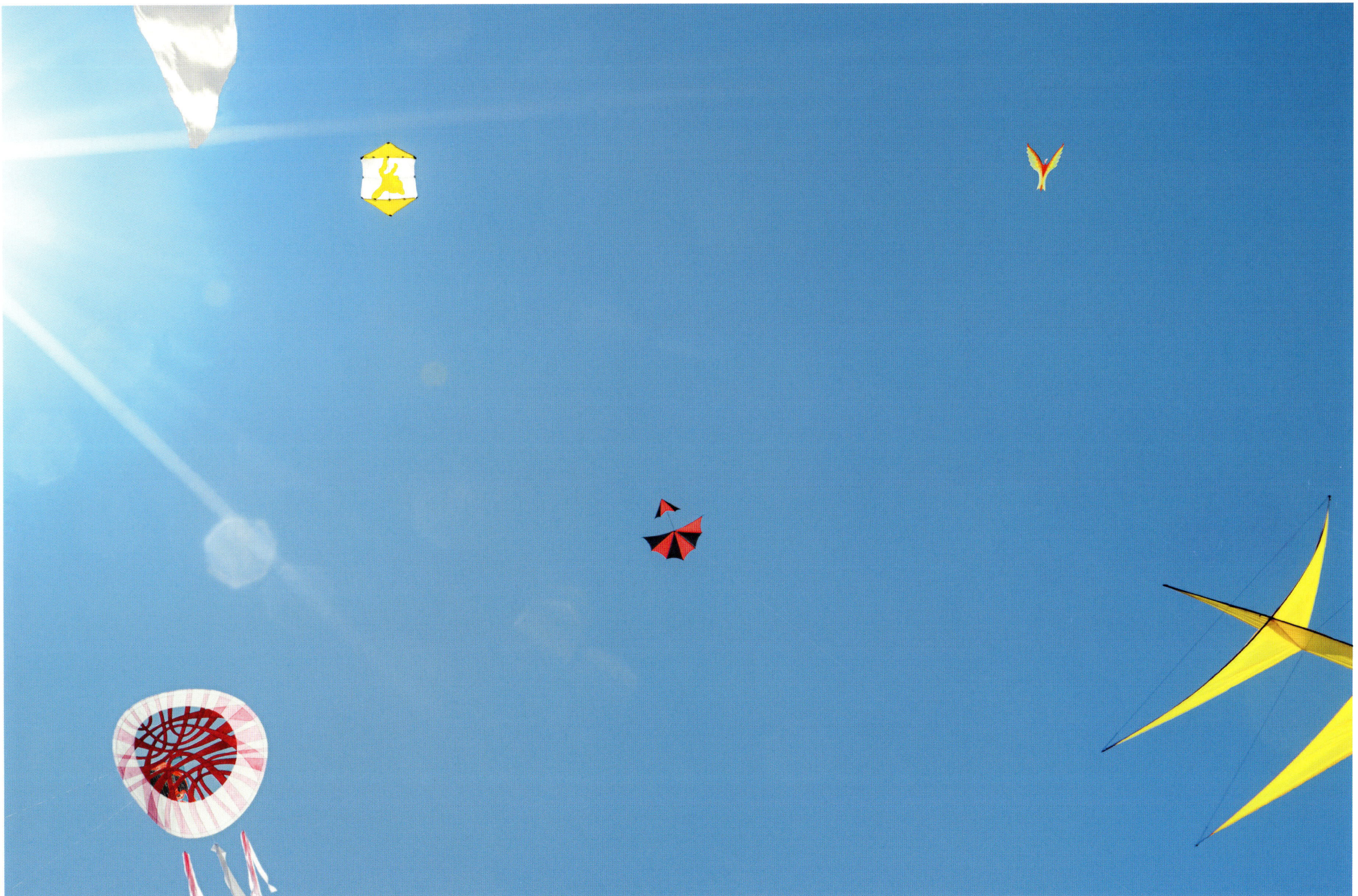

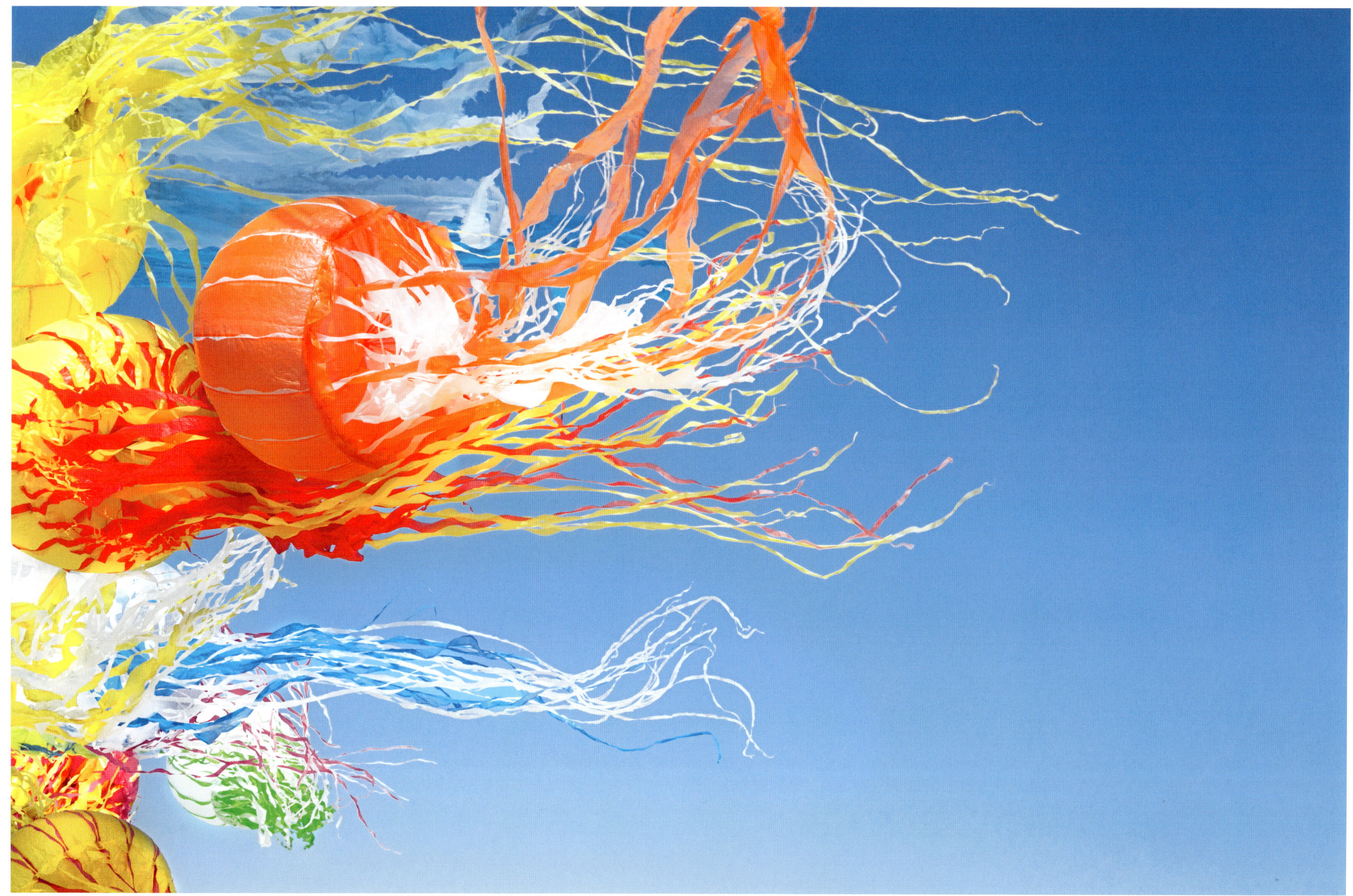

Wandering

My favorite activity is wandering with my camera, preferably in a place I don't know. Roaming on a bright and windy afternoon in the town of Syracuse, Sicily, I was drawn to a mysterious movement of color overhead. A fantastic swirl of color came from laundry hung out to dry, crisscrossing streets from balconies; intimate objects hung in a public space, animated by the wind. I made a few casual photos and later, back in my studio, I noticed in these images some potential for a human story (Who wears these jeans? Whose dress is this?). And after 30-plus years of being a black-and-white photographer, I felt the allure of ecstatic color.

Returning to the place of my original discovery, Syracuse, I began to explore the sensuality of the form and movement of hanging laundry. I photographed with my lens pointing directly overhead, making images increasingly evocative of Miro, Kandinsky, and other lyrical non-representational painters I admire. I was seeing the biomorphic resemblance of the wind-filled skirts, dishtowels, and bed linens to blooming flowers, sea creatures, amoebas, swarms of birds. Clothing became anything but quotidian. I left the horizon behind, abandoned all referential context, and used the power of the sky as a field on which to explore the painterly elements of line, form, shape, color, pattern, and texture. I was creating abstract images from the "found objects" of strangers' drying laundry. I continued my search for the perfect confluence of luminous sunshine, wind, and colorful fabrics in the seaside towns of Venice, Bari, and Catania, in Italy, as well as Havana, Cuba, and Split, Croatia.

When my husband suggested that visiting a kite festival might be an opportunity for more skyward explorations, I found myself on a Pacific beach, looking up again at a dance of floating color. Kites were now the stepping-off point for my abstractions, wind again the animating force. The sky became an ocean of plankton, jellyfish, protozoa, and a deep space of celestial bodies, constellations, and spaceships. Kites, delicate objects tethered to the earth by only the slightest of strings, spoke to me of things fragile and passing; I wanted to hold on to them if for only a moment. My desire to wander further in this ocean/outer-space of creatures, took me to festivals in Cervia, Italy; Fano Island, Denmark; and Long Beach, New Jersey.

I stand down here,
with a string in my hand,
fishing for the elusive
and unseen.

Bits of bright cloth, my only lure.

—Jack Stephens, from “Rags”

Sally Gall, New York City, New York, September 4, 2018

List of Photographs

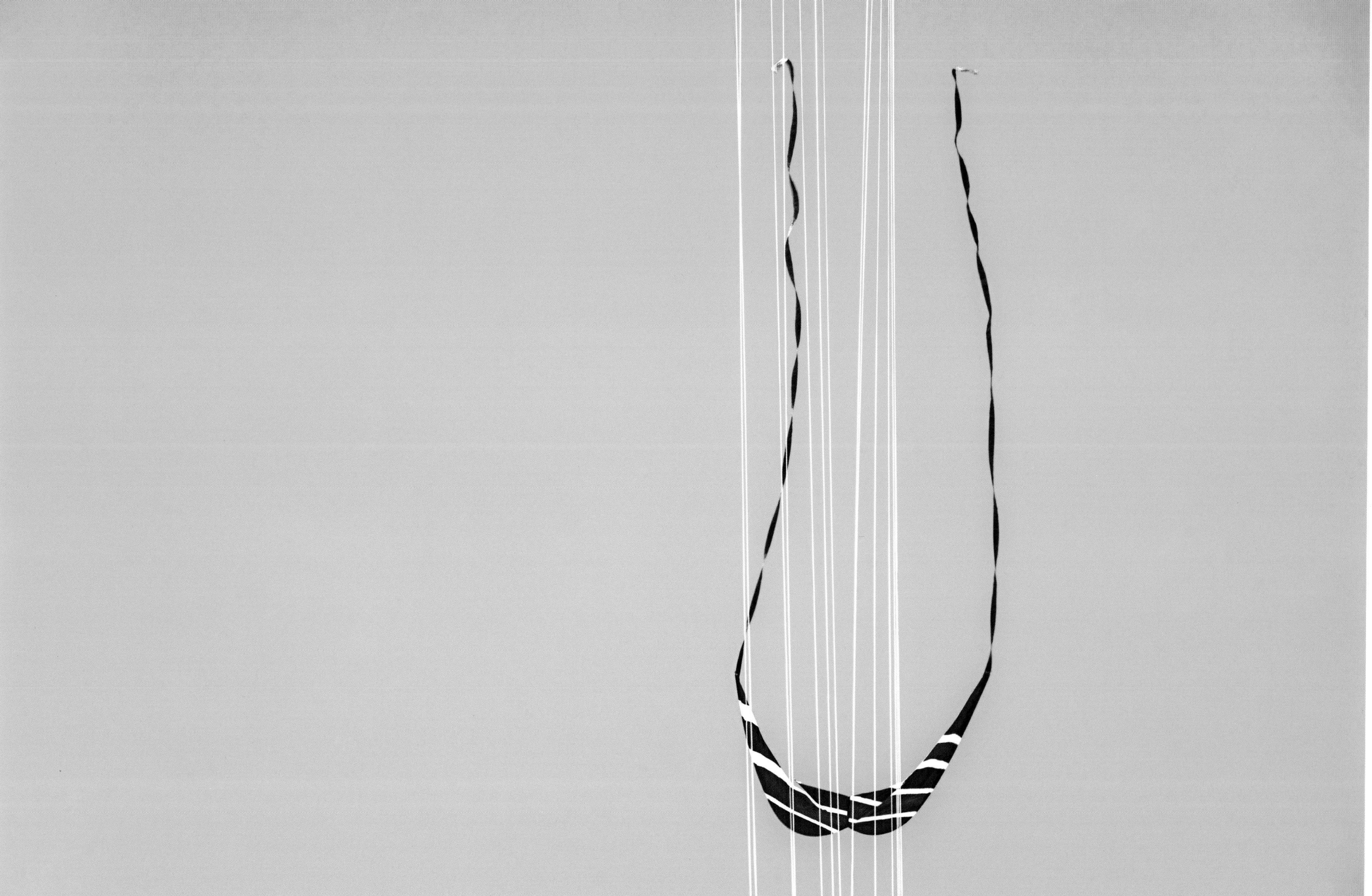

61. Blessings, 2014

63. Red Poppy, 2014

65. Migration #2, 2017

67. String Theory, 2017

69. Sylphs, 2018

71. Fantasia, 2015

73. Span, 2017

75. Aquanauts, 2017

76. Gossamer, 2017

77. Commandment, 2017

79. Composition #1, 2014

81. Diaspora, 2017

83. Birds of Paradise, 2018

85. Medusae, 2018

89. Striptease, 2018

For Jack

Acknowledgements

Thank you to the people whose expertise was critical in creating this book:

Sam Shahid, brilliant designer, for a beautiful book and for giving it a life.
Eric Fischl, painter extraordinaire, thinker, writer, for a thoughtful "Meditation."
Gerard Franciosa, My Own Color Lab, wise man and master printer, for creative technical skills and sage advice.
Additional thanks to Julie Dunham and Cooper Winterson, of My Own Color Lab, and to John MacConnell of Shahid & Company.

A special thank you to Julie Saul and Edna Cardinale, of the Julie Saul Gallery, New York, for 30 years of support and partnership.

Last but not least, thank you to my visionary husband, Jack Stephens, for endless help, support, expertise, and humor, in all things art and life.

Heavenly Creatures

Published in the United States by powerHouse Books,
a division of powerHouse Cultural Entertainment, Inc.
32 Adams Street, Brooklyn, NY 11201-1021
e-mail: info@powerHouseBooks.com
website: www.powerHouseBooks.com

First edition, 2019

Library of Congress Control Number: 2018966644

ISBN 978-1-57687-916-0

DESIGNED BY SAM SHAHID

Printing and binding by Asia Pacific Offset, Ltd.

10 9 8 7 6 5 4 3 2 1

Printed and bound in China